FOR CONSPICUOUS GALLANTRY

A BRIEF HISTORY OF THE RECIPIENTS OF THE VICTORIA CROSS FROM NOTTINGHAMSHIRE AND DERBYSHIRE

Nigel McCrery

© 1990

ISBN 0 946404 07 0

Printed and Published by
J. H. HALL & SONS LIMITED
Siddals Road, Derby
Printers and Stationers since 1831
Telephone: Derby (0332) 45218
Fax: (0332) 296146

For Gill, Luke, Emily and Rebecca
for whom it has all been for

FOREWORD

The Citations of recipients of the Victoria Cross have been recorded in many books since its inception in 1856, but the details given are usually very brief and do not give any idea of the recipient or his life before or after his award.

In his book 'Nigel McCrery' presents us with a most interesting picture of many of the men who were honoured with this decoration and he is to be congratulated for the keen interest shown in researching the lives of those award holders having connections in Nottinghamshire and Derbyshire especially.

It has been a great and rewarding experience to read these studies of local V.C's and it is hoped that others may be encouraged to add to our knowledge of this decoration.

Philip Gardner

V.C. M.C.

Captain, Royal Tank Regiment (R.A.O.)
(V.C. Tobruk, North Africa 23 November 1941)

INTRODUCTION

I have tried to make this book as accurate and interesting as possible. While researching it I was surprised to find how limited is the information on some of our Victoria Cross winners, and how contradictory the information on others. When the accounts have conflicted, I have tried to use the available sources to build up an accurate picture of the recipient, but have had to use my own judgement in this.

Wherever possible, I have used the original citation for the Victoria Cross, but occasionally I have had to alter it slightly in the interest of clarity. The rank shown at the top of each chapter is the rank held by the recipient at the time of his award.

Within the thirty-seven chapters of this book I have tried to include people with a strong Nottinghamshire or Derbyshire connection, but doubtless I will have missed some, and to them, I apologise. If any of my readers are able to supply me with any further information on local recipients I would be very glad to hear from them.

I hope that by reading this book you might be inspired to undertake further reading and research on the subject. I have only been able to give a thumbnail sketch of each man and they are all worthy of further examination.

Nigel McCrery
September 1989

A SHORT HISTORY OF THE VICTORIA CROSS

The Victoria Cross was founded by a Royal Warrant dated 29th January 1856 and was originally intended for officers and other ranks of the army and navy, who, while serving in the presence of the enemy, should have 'performed some single act of valour or devotion to their country.' It was to be awarded regardless of rank, length of service, wounds, or any other conditions whatsoever save the merit of conspicious bravery. It was held in esteem above all other decorations and awards, becoming therefore the most democratic honour in the annals of military and naval history.

Queen Victoria chose the design for the new decoration herself. It took the form of a Maltese Cross having the Royal Crest and a scroll inscribed, 'For Valour.' It was connected by a V-shaped link to a bar on the reverse of which was engraved the recipient's name, rank, number and regiment. The date on which the award was won was engraved on the reverse of the cross itself. It was required that it should not be decorative or made of any precious metal but be as intrinsically worthless as a piece of neatly designed bronze could be.

To date there have been 1,351 Crosses awarded including one to the American 'Unknown Warrior.' The first man to receive the Cross was Charles Davis Lucas, Mate, R.N., for his action in throwing a live bomb over the side of H.M.S. Hecla in the Baltic on the 21st June 1854, (almost two years before the signing of the Royal Warrant) and the last award was made to Ian John McKay, Sergeant, 3rd Battalion, The Parachute Regiment, on Mount Longdon, East Falkland, on the 12th June 1982, for destroying an enemy strong-point single handed.

There have been three instances of the Cross being awarded twice; Surgeon-Captain. A. Martin-Leake and Captain. N. G. Chavasse both of the Royal Army Medical Corps and Second-Lieutenant C. H. Upham, N.Z.E.F. The oldest man to win the award was Lieutenant W. Raynor, Bengal Veterans, who was 61 years and 10 months old when he won it. The youngest were Hospital Apprentice Fitzgibbon, Indian Medical Establishment and Drummer Flinn of the 64th Regiment. Both were aged 15 years and 3 months.

Since its inception there have been eight recorded cases of forfeiture, the recipients having been convicted of criminal offences.

In 1902, King Edward VII approved the important principle of allowing the Cross to be awarded posthumously and there were several back-dated cases of the award, such as the Crosses awarded to Lieutenants Melvill and Goghill for their actions in saving the colours during the disastrous battle at Isandlwhana. In 1911, King George V admitted native officers and men of the Indian Army to the award, which was further extended in 1920 to include the Royal Air Force, Nursing Matrons, Sisters and Nurses. He also stopped the system of forfeiture by stating that a recipient should be allowed to wear his decoration on the gallows if necessary. To date, it has not been awarded to a woman although it is available to them.

Private

FRANCIS WHEATLEY

V.C.   D.C.M.

FRENCH LEGION OF HONOUR

RIFLE BRIGADE

Francis Wheatley was born in Ruddington, Nottinghamshire in 1822 and was educated locally, prior to enlisting into the Rifle Brigade as a private soldier.

He first saw service in the South African Campaigns of 1834-53, where he served with distinction. Wheatley then travelled to Bulgaria with his Regiment, en route to the Crimea where he took part in the campaign of 1854-56, being present at the battles of the Alma and Inkerman. It was on the 12th October 1854 however during the fierce fighting in the trenches before Sebastopol that Wheatley was to win his Victoria Cross.

His citation read

'In the trenches before Sebastopol, Private Wheatley tackled a live shell that fell in the midst of the riflemen. He first tried to knock out the burning fuse with the butt of his rifle, but as he was unsuccessful in this, he deliberately picked up the shell and threw it over the parapet where it at once exploded.'

The award was gazetted on the 24th February 1857

Wheatley was decorated by Queen Victoria at the first investiture of the Victoria Cross in Hyde Park on the 26th June 1857. He was also awarded the Distinguished Conduct Medal and the French Legion of Honour for the same act of gallantry. Wheatley continued to serve with the Rifle Brigade and was later awarded the Long Service and Good Conduct Medal for his exemplary service.

On leaving the army, he became the lodge keeper at Bramshill Park, Winchfield, Hampshire for Sir William Cope Bt, a former officer of the Rifle Brigade. His health, however, had been ruined by years of campaigning and on the 21st May 1865 Francis Wheatley, V.C. died. He was buried with full military honours a few days later in the local cemetery.

His Victoria Cross, together with his campaign medals, are on display in the Regimental Museum, Winchester.

Francis Wheatley V.C.

Private

WILLIAM COFFEY

V.C. D.C.M.
FRENCH MEDAILLE MILITAIRE

BORDER REGIMENT

William Coffey was born at Conlay Hospital, Knocklong, County Limerick, Ireland on the 5th August 1829, the son of James Coffey and Mary Larkin. Little is known about his early life, other than that he gave his trade as labourer when on the 24th November 1846, at the age of seventeen, he enlisted into the 82nd (South Lancashire) Regiment.

In April 1854 Coffey transferred to the 34th Regiment (1st Battalion The Border Regiment) and sailed with them to join the army fighting in the Crimea. It was while serving in the trenches before Sebastopol that Coffey was to win his Victoria Cross.

His Citation read

'For Having On The 29th March 1855, Thrown a Lighted Shell That Fell Into The Trench, Over The Parapet'

The award was Gazetted on the 24th February 1857

For this act of gallantry Coffey was also promoted to Corporal, as well as being awarded both the Distinguished Conduct Medal, and French Medaille Militaire. He was presented with his Cross by Queen Victoria at the first investiture of the decoration at Hyde Park, London on the 26th June 1857.

Coffey also saw service during the Indian Mutiny and was involved in heavy fighting around the city of Lucknow. On the 21st December 1860, Coffey was discharged from the army and returned to civilian life. However, life outside the army did not seem to suit him and in 1861 he re-enlisted in the 75th Regiment (1st Battalion Gordon Highlanders) before transferring back to his old Regiment the 82nd Foot in July 1863. He returned to India but was declared unfit for further service and invalided home where he spent a short time in Netley Hospital. He was finally discharged from the army on the 25th August 1868 after serving 13 years and 332 days.

Undoubtedly due to his military experience Coffey soon found himself a job as a Sergeant Instructor with the militia in Sheffield. His life was to come to a tragic end when on the 13th July 1875 at the age of 46 he committed suicide at the Army Drill Hall, City Road, Sheffield. He was buried in the Roman Catholic section of Spittal Cemetery,

Chesterfield, Derbyshire.

Coffey's grave remained unmarked and forgotten for many years until the late Margaret Pratt, historian and authoress, found it while researching a book and arranged for the Border Regiment to erect a fitting monument.

Coffey's Victoria Cross and other medals are now on display in the Regimental Museum of the Border Regiment at Carlisle. There are no known photographs of William Coffey.

Russian Trenches at Sebastopol

Private

ROBERT HUMPSTON
V.C.

RIFLE BRIGADE

Like so many of the early winners of the Victoria Cross, very little is known about Robert Humpston. Information about many of these men has been either lost or forgotten.

Humpston was born in Derby in 1832 and later enlisted in the 2nd Battalion, The Rifle Brigade. He first saw service during the Crimean War, and like Wheatley and Coffey was present at the battles of the Alma and Inkermann, and also like them was to win his Victoria Cross in the trenches before Sebastopol.

His citation read

'On the 22nd April 1855 a bandsman of the 2nd Battalion was killed while getting water from a well in front of the advanced trench near the Quarries, it being impossible to make any cover near the well on account of the hardness of the ground. The man was a great favourite of his comrades and a number of them rushed out determined to drive the Russians from the rifle pits from which they had fired. Three men, Riflemen Bradshaw, Humpston and McGregor, were the first to reach and clear the pits from which only a few escaped.'

(All three men were awarded the Victoria Cross)

The award was Gazetted on the 24th February 1857

For this act of gallantry Humpston was also awarded the French Legion of Honour. He was decorated by Queen Victoria on the 26th June 1857 in Hyde Park during the first investiture of the Victoria Cross.

Humpston saw further service in India and was engaged in the suppression of the Mutiny being involved in the heavy fighting in and around the city of Lucknow. On being discharged from the army, Humpston returned to Derby where nothing further is known of his life other than he died there on 22nd December 1884.

His Victoria Cross can be seen at the Rifle Brigade's Regimental Museum, Winchester. His campaign medals are part of the Derby City Museums Collection.

Robert Humpston V.C.

Captain
WILLIAM RAYNOR
V.C.

BENGAL VETERAN ESTABLISHMENT
INDIAN ARMY

William Raynor has the distinction of being the oldest man ever to win the Victoria Cross. He was born in Plumtree, Nottinghamshire, in July 1795, the son of John and Elizabeth Raynor. He was baptised at the local church on the 10th August 1796, and educated locally.

He joined the East Indian Company in 1813 and was posted to the Bengal European Regiment serving in India. Raynor was promoted quickly becoming a Sergeant-Major in 1818 and a Sub-Conductor of Ordnance in 1819, before being commissioned from the ranks and promoted Lieutenant. This was almost unheard of within the Company's army, a substantial achievement.

He was serving with the Bengal Veterans Establishment when the great Mutiny of 1857 broke out and he was heavily engaged in its suppression. It was while defending the magazine at Delhi from the mutineers that Raynor was to win his Victoria Cross.

His Citation read

'For gallant conduct in the defence of the Magazine at Delhi, on the 11th May 1857. Of the gallant nine only four escaped. When the Magazine was blown into the air, five of them died with it — and with them died also a thousand Mutineers. Willoughby and Forrest joined a party of Europeans at the Main Guard at Delhi, so blackened as to be almost unrecognizable. Willoughby was shortly afterwards killed in an encounter with the Mutineers in a village on the way to Kutrnaul. At the attack on the fort at Rootya, Lieutenant Edward Willoughby (brother of Willoughby of the Powder Magazine), though on the sick-list, left his dhooly to join in the fight, and was killed in a daring attempt to scale the parapet. Captain Cafe and Private Thomson brought in his body, and won the Victoria Cross. The two other men of the nine who escaped were Raynor and Buckley, who, taking different directions, eventually reached Meerut in Safety.'

The award was Gazetted on the 18th June 1858

Although there is some argument as to Raynor's age at the time, it is generally held that he was 61 years and 10 months old, thus making him the oldest man ever to win the Victoria Cross.

Raynor died three years later on the 13th December 1860 at

Ferozepore, India and was buried in the local cemetery the following day. His Victoria Cross was in a private collection for many years but was purchased by the family in December 1987 for £11,000. A memorial tablet was erected over the gate of the old Magazine to commemorate Raynor and the other brave men who defended the Delhi Magazine to the last.

There are no known photographs of William Raynor.

Men of the 2nd Ghurkha Regiment outside Hindu Rao's house on the Ridge, Delhi

Sergeant

JOHN SMITH
V.C.

BENGAL SAPPERS AND MINERS

John Smith was born in February 1814 in the village of Ticknall, South Derbyshire. He was one of eight children having two brothers and five sisters. He was brought up in the village and was later apprenticed to his uncle as a cobbler. In 1837 he left the family business and joined the Honourable East India Company and began training as an engineer at Chatam. In 1839 he sailed to Delhi, later being promoted to Sergeant.

During his time in India John Smith found himself involved in much hard campaigning. In 1841 he was involved in the first Afghan war in which an entire British army was destroyed during its disastrous retreat from Kabul. He next saw service in both the Sutlej and Punjab Campaigns of 1845-49, taking part in the battles of Sobraon, Mooltan and Goojerat.

After years of war, a relative peace returned to India and Smith was able to relax with his wife and baby daughter while his talents were put to good use by the Department of Public Works in the Punjab. This peaceful interlude, however, was all too short and in 1857 a rebellion took place that came close to threatening the very existence of the British in India. The Indian Mutiny had begun in Meerut and had quickly spread. Delhi was soon in the hands of the mutineers who slaughtered its European residents before laying siege to the important cities of Lucknow and Cawnpore.

After the murder of his officer in Meerut, Smith joined the Delhi Field Force. The recapture of the fortress city of Delhi was essential to the British plans for the suppression of the mutiny, and Smith was to play an essential role in this. An important part of the attack involved the destruction of the Kashmir Gate, one of the main entrances into the city. The parties chosen for this important and dangerous task were, Lieutenants Home and Salkeld of the Bengal Engineers, Sergeants Smith and Carmichael and Corporal Burgess of the Bengal Sappers and Miners, Bugler Robert Hawthorne of the Oxford and Buckinghamshire Light Infantry and several loyal Sepoys.

The attack took place on the 14th September 1857. Home and Salkeld led the assault with Sergeants Smith and Carmichael bringing up the rear with bags of gunpowder. They moved forward under a hail of fire from the defenders, as a result of which four of the Sepoys refused to go on and it was not until Smith threatened to shoot them that two of them agreed to continue. Carmichael was shot and killed but Smith managed to reach the gate with his bag of powder before returning under heavy fire for Carmichael's bag. After Smith had arranged the fuse, Lieutenant Salkeld attempted to light it but before he had time he was shot through the leg and arm. Salkeld managed to pass the light to Burgess who was also shot. The job fell to Smith who managed to light the fuse before quickly jumping into a ditch. Before reaching the bottom however, the powder exploded blowing Smith against the ditch wall, but causing nothing more than a bruise to his leg. The plan had worked — the Kashmir Gate had been smashed and British troops entered the city.

As for the men who had taken part in the attack, both Lieutenant Home and Salkeld won the Victoria Cross. Salkeld later died from his wounds and Home was killed shortly afterwards in an accident. Sergeant Carmichael was killed in the attack and Corporal Burgess died from his wounds. Bugler Hawthorne won the Victoria Cross, as did Sergeant Smith.

His citation read

'For conspicuous gallantry in conjunction with Lieuts Home and Salkeld in the performance of the desperate duty of blowing in the Kashmir Gate of the fortress of Delhi in broad daylight and under heavy and destructive fire of musketry on the morning of the 14th September 1857 preparatory to the assault.'

The award was Gazetted on the 27th April 1858

In 1860, Smith was commissioned ensign. His days of campaigning however were over and on the 26th June 1864, while on a visit to Jullundur, he caught dysentry and died. He was buried the following day with full military honours in the Artillery Cemetery at Jullundur, where his grave can still be seen.

The Kashmir Gate still stands, and on the wall is written the name of John Smith V.C. along with the others that took part in the assault. His Victoria Cross is now in a private collection. There are no known photographs of John Smith.

The Kashmir Gate, Delhi

Private
BERNARD McQUIRT
V.C.

95th FOOT
(NOTTINGHAMSHIRE AND DERBYSHIRE REGIMENT)

Private Bernard McQuirt was the first man of the Nottinghamshire and Derbyshire Regiment to win the Victoria Cross. He was born in Donacloney, near Lurgan, Co. Armagh, in 1829. Little is known of his early life other than on his enlistment into the 95th Regiment at Lurgan on the 3rd of October 1853 he gave his age as 25 and his trade as labourer. Although there are no known photographs of McQuirt, records describe him as a small man, being only 5ft 6½ inches tall, with brown hair and eyes and a fresh complexion.

McQuirt first saw service during the Crimean War and was present in the trenches before Sebastopol, taking part in the final assault against the fortified Russian positions. After the Crimea, McQuirt was posted to the Cape of Good Hope and it was while en route to the Cape that news of the Indian Mutiny reached the Regiment. They were diverted to Bombay, landing in India on the 30th October 1857, where they joined the Central Indian Field Force. The 95th soon found themselves in the thick of the fighting. They marched and fought their way over 2,500 miles of jungle and desert and took part in no less than 14 actions. This alone stands as a marvel of military endurance and achievement.

It was during this campaign on the 6th January 1858 that the left wing of the regiment with four officers, 108 other ranks, two guns and two companies of the 10th Bombay Infantry attacked the fortified village of Rowa which was held by a large party of mutineers. The 10th Bombay Infantry attacked the right flank of the village whilst the 95th made a frontal assault assisted by a Regiment of native auxiliaries. These auxiliaries did great execution among the mutineers with their bows. (In fact, these natives were head-hunters and could be seen later in the day returning from the village with bunches of the mutineers' heads tied together by their hair). The village was captured and destroyed. It was during this action that McQuirt saved the life of Captain McGowan, commanding officer of the 10th Native Infantry and won his Victoria Cross.

His citation read

'For gallant conduct on the 6th January 1858 at the capture of Rowa when he was severely and dangerously wounded in a hand-to-hand fight with three men, of whom he killed one and wounded another. He received five sabre cuts and a musket shot in this service.'

The award was Gazetted on the 11th November 1859

After a term of hospitalisation to recover from his wounds, McQuirt returned to England and on the 4th January 1860 he attended Windsor Castle to be presented with his Cross by Queen Victoria. So shocked was the Queen at the sabre wounds to McQuirt's head that she wrote in her journal that evening that she had feared to speak to him.

McQuirt was invalided out of the army as a result of his wounds. He returned to Ireland and resided in Belfast where he drew his army pension until his death at 72 Urney Street, Belfast on the 5th October 1888, aged 50. He was buried without ceremony two days later in a common grave. For many years the location of McQuirt's grave was unknown. However due to work done by the Regiment and a Metropolitan Police Officer, P.C. Ron Biddle, it was discovered in the Belfast City Cemetery a few years ago. McQuirt's Victoria Cross and campaign medals have, alas, been lost.

Dead Mutineers outside the 'Secundra Bagh,' Lucknow

Captain

SIR HENRY WILMOT, BART
V.C. K.C.B.

RIFLE BRIGADE

Henry Wilmot was born in Chaddesden, Derbyshire on the 3rd February 1831, the second son of Sir Sacheverel Wilmot, Bart, Deputy-Lieutenant and High Sheriff of Derbyshire. He was educated at Rugby School and joined the 43rd (Oxfordshire and Buckinghamshire) Light Infantry in 1849. In 1851 he transferred to the 2nd Battalion The Rifle Brigade and saw service with them during the Crimean war, being present in the trenches before Sebastopol.

In July 1857 he sailed for India where he became Deputy Judge Advocate and was heavily engaged in the suppression of the Indian Mutiny. It was during the heavy fighting in and around the besieged city of Lucknow on the 11th March 1858 that Captain Wilmot was to win his Victoria Cross.

His citation read

'*For conspicuous gallantry at Lucknow on the 11th March 1858. Capt. Wilmot's company was engaged with a large body of the enemy near the Iron Bridge. That officer found himself at the end of a street with only four of his men and opposed by a considerable body. One of the four was shot through both legs and became utterly helpless; the two other men lifted him up, and although Private Hawkes was severely wounded, he carried him for a considerable distance, exposed to the fire of the enemy, Captain Wilmot firing with the men's rifles and covering the retreat of the party.*'

The award was Gazetted on the 24th December 1858

Captain Wilmot next saw service during the Second China war of 1860-61, and was appointed Judge Advocate General to the expeditionary force. He finally retired from the army with the rank of Major in 1861 and returned home to Derby. He entered politics and became active in the Conservative Party. He was elected to Parliament for the old South Derbyshire Division in a closely-run election in 1868. He was re-elected in 1874 and again in 1880. Due to the death of his brother without an heir Sir Henry was obliged to give up his political career to become the 5th Baron Chaddesden, although he maintained a keen interest in local politics. He became a K.C.B. in 1897.

Sir Henry died at "Chaddesden," Bournemouth on the 7th April 1901. His medals were presented to the Rifle Brigade's Regimental Museum, Winchester by his grand-nephew, Sir Robert Wilmot, Bart in 1964 and are now on public display.

18

Sir Henry Wilmot V.C.

Private

SAMUEL MORLEY
V.C.

THE MILITARY TRAIN

Samuel Morley was born in 1829 and baptised at St. Mary's Church, Radcliffe-on-Trent, Nottinghamshire. He began his military career serving with the 8th Hussars, being sent out to the Crimea in September, 1855 as a replacement due to the regiment's heavy casualties. He returned to England with the regiment the following year and transferred to the Military Train.

Samuel Morley was, to say the least, a 'bit of a lad' during his service. His name appears no less than sixteen times in the Regimental defaulters book. He was court martialled twice and served two terms of imprisonment, being prone to going absent without leave. He was, however, one of the bravest men ever to serve with the British Army.

Morley next saw service in India, travelling with his Regiment to help suppress the Mutiny of 1857. It was during this campaign that Morley was to win his Victoria Cross.

His citation read

'*Samuel Morley, Private 201, 2nd Battalion Military Train. On the evacuation of Aximghur by Kooer Singh's Army on the 15th April 1858, a squadron of the Military Train and half a troop of Horse Artillery were sent in pursuit. Upon overtaking them and coming into action with their rearguard, a squadron of the 3rd Sikh Cavalry (also detached in pursuit) and a troop of the Military Train were ordered to charge, when Lieut. Hamilton, who commanded the Sikhs, was unhorsed and immediately surrounded by the enemy who commenced cutting him and hacking him whilst on the ground. Private Samuel Morley, seeing the predicament that Lieutenant Hamilton was in, although his own horse had been shot from under him, immediately, and most gallantly, rushed up on foot to his assistance and in conjunction with Farrier Murphy, who has already received the Victoria Cross for the same thing, cut down one of the Sepoys and fought over Lieutenant Hamilton's body until further assistance came up and thereby was the means of saving Lieutenant Hamilton from being killed on the spot*'.

The award was Gazetted on the 7th August 1860

Morley's award was not as straightforward as most and is one of the more colourful cases in the complex history of the Cross. It will have been

20

noticed by reading Morley's citation that as well as Morley, Farrier Murphy also defended the wounded officer. Murphy was awarded the Victoria Cross for this action (London Gazette dated 27th May 1859) but at first Morley was not. On returning to England, Morley learnt of Murphy's award and was more than a little aggrieved. In May 1860 he complained to General Lord Paget C.B. who was making his half-yearly inspection at Aldershot. General Paget ordered an immediate enquiry. The evidence was collected and Morley's claim to the Victoria Cross was upheld, and on the 9th November 1860 he received his Cross from Queen Victoria at Home Park, Windsor.

Samuel Morley was discharged from the army in 1870 after serving 14 years 249 days, and returned to his home at Radcliffe-on-Trent. The people of Nottingham were very proud of their Victoria Cross winner and soon found Morley regular employment at the local gas works. He continued in his civilian life settling down to bring up his family and died aged 59 on 16th June 1888, whilst residing at 13 Garnett Street, Nottingham. Again the city of Nottingham rallied around and paid for an inscribed head-stone which can still be seen in the General Cemetery, Nottingham.

His Victoria Cross and campaign medals were missing for many years but are now in the hands of the Royal Corps of Transport having been presented to them by The Institute of Medals, in 1964.

Samuel Morley V.C.

Colour-Sergeant

ANTHONY BOOTH

V.C.

SOUTH STAFFORDSHIRE REGIMENT

Anthony Booth was born in Carrington, Nottingham on the 21st April 1846. He was educated locally before being apprenticed to a local tailor. The life of a tailor, however, did not appear to suit Booth and orrthe 28th October, 1864 he enlisted in the 2nd Battalion The South Staffordshire Regiment as a private soldier. Whilst serving with the regiment his habits were described as both regular and temperate and his conduct exemplary. This description however seems a little exaggerated as he was a man with a quick temper and a sharp tongue, these traits getting him reduced in rank on more than one occasion.

He saw much service abroad, but it was during the South African Campaign of 1878-79, more usually termed the Zulu War, that he was to show his full potential. It was during this campaign that the British army was to suffer its greatest defeat at the hands of native regiments and later achieve one of its greatest victories. At Isandhlwana five companies of the 1/24 Foot, one company of the 2/24th (South Wales Borderers), together with 59 artillerymen, a few engineers and native followers (a total of approximately 1,329 men) were annihilated by Zulu impis. The British army lost more officers at Isandhlwana than they had at Waterloo. At Rorke's Drift, however, a garrison of 139 men who were guarding the sick and the wounded were attacked by approximately 3,000 Zulus, and during its epic defence no fewer than 11 Victoria Crosses were won and the Zulus forced to retire.

On the 12th March 1879 the Zulus launched a successful surprise attack on a British encampment on the Intombi River. It was here that Captain Moriarty and 55 men of the South Staffordshire Regiment were to lose their lives and Sergeant Booth was to win his Victoria Cross.

His citation read

'For his gallant conduct on the 12th March 1879 during the Zulu attack on the Intombi River in having when condiserably outnumbered by the enemy, rallied a few men on the South bank of the river, and covered the retreat of 15 soldiers and others over a distance of three miles. The officer commanding the 80th Regiment reports that, had it not been for the coolness displayed by this non-commissioned officer, not one man would have escaped.'

The award was Gazetted on the 23rd February 1880

Sergeant Booth was originally recommended for the Distinguished Conduct Medal but Booth's outstanding bravery so impressed Lord Chelmsford, the officer commanding, that it was changed to the Victoria Cross. He was presented with his Cross by Queen Victoria at Windsor Castle on the 26th June 1880. As well as several other gifts from the people of South Africa he was also presented with a silver revolver from the officers of the Regiment.

Sergeant Booth continued to serve with the Regiment until 1885 when he transfered to the 1st Volunteer Battalion The South Staffordshire Regiment as an instructor. He finally retired from the army in 1889 having served a total of 33 years and 182 days.

He never settled to civilian life and died the following year on the 8th December 1890 while residing at Brierley Hill, Staffordshire and was buried with full military honours. His medals are now in the hands of the Regiment, which is where Sergeant Anthony Booth V.C. would have wanted them to be.

Anthony Booth V.C.

Quartermaster Sergeant

WILLIAM MARSHALL
V.C.

19th HUSSARS

William Thomas Marshall was born at Newark, Nottinghamshire on the 5th December 1854. He was educated privately before joining the 19th Hussars on the 20th July 1873. He first saw service in the Egyptian campaign of 1882 and took part in the battle of Tel-el-Kebir on the 13th September 1882, when the Egyptian forces under the command of Arabi Pasha were routed by the British army and later surrendered unconditionally. Marshall continued to serve in Egypt and took part in the Sudan Expedition of 1884 where he was involved in both the battles of El-Teb (29th February 1884) and Tamaai (13th March 1884). It was during the battle of El-Teb that Marshall was to win his Victoria Cross.

His Citation read

'For his conspicuous bravery during the Cavalry charge at El-Tab on the 29th February 1884 in bringing Lieutenant-Colonel Barrow, 19th Hussars, out of the action, that officer having been severely wounded and his horse killed, was on the ground surrounded by the enemy, when Quartermaster Sergeant Marshall, who stayed behind with him, seized his hand and dragged him through the enemy back to the Regiment. Had Lieutenant-Colonel Barrow been left behind, he would have been killed.'

The award was Gazetted on the 21st May 1884

Sergeant Marshall was to have the unusual distinction of being presented with his Cross twice. He first received his Cross from Colonel A. G. Webster, commanding the 19th Hussars in Egypt in May 1884 and then again from the Queen at Windsor Castle on the 3rd July 1884. (The first Cross having been handed in).

He was commissioned as Lieutenant and Quartermaster on the 20th January 1885 before travelling to South Africa to take part in the Boer war of 1899-1900. Lieutenant Marshall took part in the operations around Natal, including the actions at Lombards Kop, the defence of Ladysmith and Laing's Nek. On the 20th January 1907 Marshall retired from the army and settled in Fife, Scotland, where he became secretary of the Fife County Territorial Forces Association. During the First World War he was mentioned in despatches, 'for valuable service rendered in connection with the war.'

He died at his home in Kirkaldy, Fife, on the 11th September 1920 and

24

was buried with full military honours. Marshall's Victoria Cross and campaign medals were sold at auction in 1964 for the then record sum of £900. They are now in the possession of the Regiment.

William Marshall V.C. .Courtesy of The Imperial War Museum Q 80590

Captain

HENRY SINGLETON PENNELL
V.C.

NOTTINGHAMSHIRE AND DERBYSHIRE REGIMENT

Henry Singleton Pennell was born on the 18th June, 1874 at Dawlish, Devon. He was educated at Eastbourne College where he was described as a bright, intelligent boy and a keen sportsman. In 1893 he was commissioned into the Nottinghamshire and Derbyshire Regiment as a 2nd Lieutenant, being promoted Lieutenant in 1896. Pennell first saw service with the Regiment in India as part of the Tirah Field Force.

It was during this campaign on the 20th October 1987, while in action on the Dargai Heights, that Pennell was to win his Victoria Cross.

His citation read

'Henry Singleton Pennell, Lieutenant, Nottingham and Derbyshire Regiment. This officer during the attack on the Dargai Heights, on the 20th October 1897, when Captain W. E. G. Smith of the Derbyshire Regiment was struck down, ran to his assistance and made two distinct attempts under a perfect hail of bullets to carry and drag him back under cover, and only desisted when he found that he was dead.'

The award was Gazetted on the 20th May 1898

He was decorated with his cross by Colonel Dowse at Bareilly, North West India on the 2nd September 1898. Lieutenant Pennell also received the Indian Medal (1895-1902) with two bars. In 1898 he again saw action in the South African Campaign of 1899-1902, (Boer War) this time attached to the West Yorkshire Regiment serving with the Natal Field Force. He was involved in the operations for the relief of Ladysmith and was present during the battles of Colenso and Spion Kop, and during the bloody fighting for the Tugela, which culminated in the capture of Pieter's Hill, he was seriously wounded. Pennell was mentioned in despatches twice during this campaign and received the Queen's South Africa medal with five clasps.

He returned home in 1900 and was promoted to company commander and later specially selected to attend the Staff College. On graduating he was posted to a staff appointment.

It was a combination of Pennell's love of sports and cool courage that eventually led to his death. On the 19th January 1907, while on the toboggan run at St. Mortizdorf, Switzerland, a serious accident occurred in which the brave Captain was killed. Pennell was the epitome of the British

26

Officer at the time of Empire; brave, strong and intelligent. We can only speculate as to what heights his career would have reached had it not been cut so tragically short.

Captain Pennell's Victoria Cross and campaign medals can now be seen in the Nottinghamshire and Derbyshire's Regimental Museum, Nottingham Castle.

Henry Singleton Pennell V.C.

Corporal
HARRY CHURCHILL BEET
V.C.

NOTTINGHAMSHIRE AND DERBYSHIRE REGIMENT

Harry Churchill Beet was born at Brackendale Farm, Bingham, Nottinghamshire on the 1st April, 1873 and was educated locally before joining the Nottinghamshire and Derbyshire Regiment on the 18th February 1892. He sailed with the Regiment to India in 1894 and was engaged in the Punjab campaign between 1897-98, for which he received the campaign medal with two clasps.

He next saw service in the South African war of 1899-02 (Boer War) and it was during this campaign that he was to win the Victoria Cross.

His citation read

'Harry Churchill Beet, Corporal 1st Battalion Mounted Infantry. At Wakkerstroom on the 22nd April 1900 No. 2 Mounted Infantry Company 1st Battalion Derbyshire Regiment with two squadrons Imperial Yeomanry had to retire from near a farm, under a ridge held by Boers. Corporal Burnett, Imperial Yeomanry was left on the ground wounded, and Corporal Beet seeing him remained behind and placed him under cover, bound up his wounds and prevented the Boers from coming to the farm till dark, when Dr. Wilson, Imperial Yeomanry, came to the wounded man's assistance. The retirement was carried out under a very heavy fire, and Corporal Beet was exposed to fire during the whole afternoon.'

The award was Gazetted on the 12th February 1901

He was decorated by The Duke of York (later King George V) at Natal on the 4th August 1901 and was later promoted to Sergeant by Lord Kitchener for his service in the field. In 1903 he left the regular army, but continued his military career in the reserve, serving with the South Notts. Hussars until 1905. He emigrated to Canada with his family the following year.

At the outbreak of the First World War, Harry Beet V.C. enlisted into the Saskatchewan Light Horse seeing service with them in Europe. He was commissioned in January 1916. At the end of the war he retired from the army with the honourable rank of Captain, and returned to Canada.

At the outbreak of the Second World War Beet joined the army yet again, this time serving with the 110th Infantry Reserve Company, The Veteran Guard of Canada, but was discharged due to his age in March 1942. A small thing like age however was not going to stop Beet and he joined the Royal Canadian Mounted Police and spent the rest of the war guarding Japanese prisoners of war in British Columbia.

Beet finally died at Rupert, Vancouver, British Columbia, Canada on the 10th January 1946 and was buried with full military honours at Vancouver Veterans Cemetery. His Victoria Cross and other campaign medals can be seen in the Regimental Museum at Nottingham Castle.

Harry Churchill Beet V.C.   Courtesy of The Imperial War Museum Q 80472

Private

WILLIAM BEES

V.C.

NOTTINGHAMSHIRE AND DERBYSHIRE REGIMENT

William Bees was born at Loughborough, Leicestershire on the 12th September, 1872 the son of William and Jane Bees. He received his education at a local board school before enlisting into the 1st Battalion The Nottinghamshire and Derbyshire Regiment at Normanton Barracks on the 7th March 1890.

During his military career Bees saw service on the Indian Frontier, being involved in the Tirah Campaign of 1897-98 for which he received the medal and clasp. He next saw service during the South African War (Boer War) of 1899-1902, and it was during this campaign that Bees was to win his Victoria Cross.

His Citation read

'W. Bees Private, 1st Battalion the Derbyshire Regt. Private Bees was one of the Maxim-Gun detachment which at Moedwil on the 30th September 1901 had six men hit out of nine. Hearing his wounded comrades asking for water, he went forward, under a heavy fire, to a spruit held by the Boers, about 500 yards ahead of the gun, and brought back a kettle full of water. In going and returning he had to pass within 100 yards of some rocks, also held by the Boers, and the kettle which he was carrying was hit by several bullets.'

The award was Gazetted on the 17th December 1901

Private Bees was decorated with his cross by Lord Kitchener, then Commandant at Rustenburg, in the Transvaal on the 30th July 1902, and he was also promoted to Corporal.

Corporal Bees' act of gallantry captured the British public's imagination to such a degree that a well known song writer of the day, Mary Bradford was inspired to compose a ballad called 'The Old Kettle', which was based on Bees act of gallantry and became a very popular music hall song of its day. William Bees was discharged from the army on the 18th September 1902. The following year he married a local girl at All Saints Church, Loughborough, they had two children both of whom died in infancy.

In October 1914 at the outbreak of the First World War, Bees enlisted into Kitchener's Army but was discharged due to ill-health. In 1915 he again tried to join up and re-enlisted into the Nottinghamshire and Derbyshire Regiment being later transferred into the Durham Light

Infantry. After serving for over a year with the Regiment he was again discharged from the army. They say old soldiers never die and Bees enlisted again, this time joining the Royal Army Service Corps in 1918. He served with the Corps until the end of the war being finally demobilised on the 6th February 1919.

After the war Bees was employed as a road-sweeper by the Coalville Urban District Council. He was a well known and popular local figure who attended many functions, including a garden party at Buckingham Palace given by King George V and the famous V.C. dinner held in the House of Lords in November 1929. It was during this dinner that Bees spoke to and became friendly with the Prince of Wales. (Later Edward VIII).

During his later life William Bees V.C. was to gain national attention when he was summoned for having no dog licence. During his appearance in court the magistrate asked Bees why he had failed to purchase a licence. Bees replied that he could not afford a licence and did not have the heart to have his dog destroyed. He was fined seven shillings and a penny which he was ordered to pay at one shilling a week. Such was the public outcry against the winner of a Victoria Cross having been allowed to fall on such hard times, that money was sent to him from all over the country and his fine was paid by an anonymous benefactor who also purchased a dog licence for him. He was also given a life pension of ten shillings a week by the Royal British Legion. Due to the publicity surrounding the episode Bees' Kings South African medal, which had been lost for many years, was returned to him by a woman in Rugby who had found it lying in the street several years before.

William Bees V.C. finally died aged 65 at his home in Margaret Street, Coalville on the 20th June 1938 and was buried with full military honours.

William Bees' medals were presented to the Nottinghamshire and Derbyshire Regiment by his wife Sarah on the 15th October 1938, and are now in display in the Regimental Museum at Nottingham Castle.

William Bees V.C.

Corporal

CHARLES ERNEST GARFORTH
V.C.

15th KINGS HUSSARS

Charles Ernest Garforth was born at Willesden Green, London on the 23rd October 1891 and was educated at Green Hill School near Harrow. On leaving school he worked for a short time at 'Joiners' book shop, Harrow before joining the 9th Battalion The Middlesex Regiment, (Territorial Forces) in 1909. In 1911 Garforth transferred to the 15th (The Kings) Hussars and after a period of training joined the Regiment at Potchefstroom, South Africa, where he remained until 1913.

On the 16th August 1914 at the outbreak of the First World War Garforth, who had by now been promoted Corporal, sailed with his Regiment to France and was soon heavily engaged in the fighting. He took part in the Battle of Mons and fought throughout the famous retreat. He was also involved in the battles of the Marne, Aisne and the first battle of Ypres. During this time Garforth was recommended for the Victoria Cross no less than three times.

His Citation read

'On the 23rd August 1914, Garforth's troop was fighting a rearguard action near Harmignies; the troop was nearly surrounded, and was held up by a wire fence. Corporal Garforth cut this wire fence, in spite of the fact that the Germans had turned machine-gun fire on to it, with the express purpose of preventing it being cut. This action allowed the troop to make a gallop for safety. Again on the 6th September 1914, near Dammartin, Corporal Garforth was out on patrol when the patrol came under heavy fire and was forced to retire. Sergeant Scatterfield's horse was shot, and the Sergeant became trapped under it. Garforth went forward under heavy fire and pulled the Sergeant from under his horse, and took him to a place of safety. The following day (7th September) while on patrol, Sergeant Lewis had his horse shot, and was left on foot and under heavy machine-gun fire. Garforth drew the fire of the machine-guns onto himself by engaging them with his rifle, thus enabling the Sergeant to get away under cover.'

The award was gazetted on the 16th November 1914

Shortly after winning his Cross Garforth was made prisoner of war. On the 13th October, 1914 while he was on patrol with his troop at La Bassee-Ypres, it was surrounded by Germans and in the battle that followed the officer together with seven troopers was killed. Corporal Garforth held out until all his ammunition had been expended at which time he was forced to surrender. He was at first interned at Hamelin-on-Weser but was later transferred to Bohmte. While in captivity he made three attempts to escape but was recaptured on each occasion at the German-Dutch frontier line, being too weak through exhaustion and lack of food to avoid the guards.

At the end of the war he was repatriated to England but later rejoined his regiment and served with them as part of the army of occupation in Germany. He was decorated by King George V at Buckingham Palace on the 19th December 1918, over four years after he had won his Cross. He was promoted to Sergeant and continued to serve with the regiment in Ireland and at Tidworth. In 1919 he was married and had two children. He was finally discharged from the army in 1922.

He settled to civilian life and found employment with the Security Police at Chilwell Ordnance Depot, Nottinghamshire. During the Second World War he served as an A.R.P. instructor for British Celanese at Spondon with whom he remained after the war as a warehouseman.

Charles Garforth V.C. died at his home in Beeston, Nottinghamshire on the 1st July 1973 aged 81 years. As a lasting tribute to his bravery the lead tank of 'A' Squadron 15th/19th The Kings Royal Hussars will always bear the name of 'Garforth V.C.'

Charles Ernest Garforth V.C. and Wife
Courtesy of The Imperial War Museum HU 48670

Corporal

WILFRED DOLBY FULLER

V.C.

RUSSIAN ORDER OF ST. GEORGE

GRENADIER GUARDS

Wilfred Dolby Fuller was born at East Kirkby, Greasley, Nottinghamshire on the 28th July 1893. He was educated locally after which he found employment as a miner at the Crown Farm Colliery, Mansfield. He enlisted into the 1st Battalion the Grenadier Guards at Nottingham on the 30th December 1911 at the age of eighteen.

He fought with the Guards during the First World War and was promoted to Lance-Corporal. He won his Victoria Cross at Neuve Chapelle, France on the 12th March 1915.

His Citation read

'For the most conspicuous bravery at Neuve Chapelle on the 12th March 1915. Seeing a party of the enemy endeavoring to escape along a communication trench, he ran towards them and killed the leading man with a bomb; the remainder (nearly 50) finding no means of evading his bombs, surrendered to him. Lance Corporal Fuller was quite alone at the time.'

The award was Gazetted on the 19th April 1915

He was decorated by King George V at Buckingham Palace on the 4th June 1915. He was also given a civic reception at Mansfield and presented with an illuminated address and a gold watch by the Mayor. Such was Fuller's popularity that he was kept in England and employed on recruiting duties. On the 29th September 1915 while in Sheffield he was again decorated by the King this time with the Russian Order of St. George, (3rd Class) for distinguished service in the field and was promoted to Corporal.

On the 31st October 1916 Wilfred Fuller was discharged from the army as medically unfit. He moved to Frome, Somerset and there he joined the local Constabularly with whom he continued to serve until he was forced to retire in July 1940 due to ill health.

Wilfred Fuller V.C. died on the 22nd November 1947 aged 55 years and was buried at Christ Church, Frome, Somerset with full military honours. A hundred Guardsmen and over sixty Police officers attended the funeral. His Victoria Cross and campaign medals are now in private hands.

N.B: Since the writing of the book, the regiment have received Fuller's V.C. and Campaign Medals.

Wilfred Dolby Fuller V.C.   Courtesy of The Guards Museum, London

Private

JACOB RIVERS
V.C.

NOTTINGHAMSHIRE AND DERBYSHIRE REGIMENT

Jacob Rivers was born on the 17th November 1881 at House 4, Court 12, Wideyard, Brides Gate, Derby and was one of three sons born to Mrs Adeline Rivers. Little is known of his early life other than, his family were poor, Jacob's father having died at the early age of forty-one, leaving his mother to bring up the family on her own. It is not surprising, then, that as soon as they were old enough the brothers left home and on the 3rd June 1899, at the age of eighteen, Jacob enlisted into the Royal Scots Fusiliers.

He served with the Fusiliers in India for seven years before being discharged to the reserve on the 3rd June 1907, where he served for a further five years. On leaving the army he found employment as a labourer on the ballast trains for the Midlands Railway Company at Derby where he worked until the outbreak of the First World War. On the 18th August 1914, Jacob re-enlisted into the army, this time joining the Nottinghamshire and Derbyshire Regiment. He was posted to the 1st Battalion and because of his previous military training, was sent to France with one of the first drafts.

Jacob Rivers saw much heavy fighting with the Regiment and it was at Neuve Chapelle on the 12th March 1915, that Jacob Rivers was to win his Victoria Cross.

His Citation read

'For the most conspicuous bravery at Neuve Chapelle on the 12th March 1915 when he, on his own initiative, crept to within a few yards of a large number of the enemy who were massed on the flank of an advanced company of his battalion and hurled bombs on them. His action caused the enemy to retire, and so relieved the situation. Private Rivers performed a second act of great bravery on the same day, similar to the first mentioned- again causing the enemy to retire. He was killed on this occasion.'

The award was gazetted on the 28th April 1915

Jacob Rivers' body was never recovered due to the heavy fighting at the time and he has no known grave. His name, however, is commemorated on the La Tourt Memorial, France.

Jacob's Victoria Cross was presented to his mother by King George V at Buckingham Palace on the 29th November 1916. So proud were the people of Derbyshire at the award of the Victoria Cross to Jacob that on the 23rd March 1923 they made his mother a Freeman, an honour she shared with Earl Haig and the Duke of Devonshire. Mrs. Rivers died on the 1st March 1937 and was buried in the Nottingham Road Cemetery, Derby where a memorial not only to her but to her brave son Jacob now stands.

The Victoria Cross and Campaign medals won by Jacob during the First World War were presented to the regiment in accordance with the wishes of Adeline Rivers at a civic reception on the 7th April 1937 and are now on display at the Regimental Museum at Nottingham Castle.

Jacob Rivers V.C.

Corporal

WALTER RICHARD PARKER

V.C.

ROYAL MARINE LIGHT INFANTRY

Walter Richard Parker was born at 5 Agnes Street, Grantham, Lincolnshire on the 20th September 1881, the son of Richard and Kate Parker. While he was still young the family moved to London and he was educated at the local school in Kentish Town. The family returned to the Midlands and settled in Stapleford, Nottinghamshire, where Walter found employment as a coremaker at the local Iron Works at Stanton. During this time Walter married Olivia Orchard, the daughter of the local station master, and their marriage produced three daughters.

On the 7th September 1914, shortly after the outbreak of the First World War, Walter enlisted into the Royal Marine Light Infantry and was attached to the Portsmouth Division. After the completion of his training he sailed for Egypt and then on to the Dardanelles and it was during the fierce fighting in Gallipoli that he was to win his Victoria Cross.

His Citation read

'On the night of the 30th April/1st May 1915, a message asking for ammunition, water and medical supplies was received from an isolated fire-trench at Gaba Tepe.

A Party of non-commissioned officers and men were detailed to carry water and ammunition, and, in response to a call for a volunteer from among the stretcher-bearers, Parker at once came forward; he had, during the previous three days, displayed conspicuous bravery and energy under fire whilst in charge of the Battalion stretcher bearers.

Several men had already been killed in a previous attempt to bring assistance to the men holding the fire trench. To reach the trench it was necessary to traverse an area at least four hundred yards wide which was completely exposed and swept by rifle fire. It was already daylight when the party emerged from shelter and at once one of the men was wounded. Parker organised a stretcher party and then, going on alone, succeeded in reaching the fire-trench, all the water and ammunition carriers being either killed or wounded.

After his arrival he rendered assistance to the wounded in the trench, displaying extreme courage and remaining cool and collected in very trying circumstances. The trench had finally to be evacuated and Parker helped to remove and to attend the wounded, although he himself was seriously wounded during this operation.'

The award was Gazetted on the 22nd June 1917

He was decorated by King George V at Buckingham Palace on the 21st July 1917. The unusual delay of two years between Parker's act of gallantry and the award of the Cross was due to poor communication between the officers under whom he served. As well as the Victoria Cross, Corporal Parker was invited to Forton Barracks where he was presented with an inscribed marble and gilt clock, together with a cheque, and Mrs. Parker was presented with a gold regimental brooch. The inscription on the clock read, 'Presented to Corporal W. R. Parker V.C. by the Portsmouth Division R.M.L.I. (all ranks) as a mark of appreciation of his gallant conduct at Gallipoli 1915.'

Corporal Parker was discharged from the Royal Marines on the 17th June 1917, due to the wounds he had received at the time he won his Cross. He returned to civilian life and found employment as a munitions worker at the Chilwell Ordnance Factory and became the president of the Royal British Legion club at Stapleford.

Walter Richard Parker V.C. died at his home on Derby Road, Stapleford on the 28th November 1936, aged 56 years, and was buried with full military honours in the local cemetery. His Victoria Cross together with his campaign medals is now in the possession of the Royal Marines.

Walter Richard Parker V.C.

Corporal

JAMES UPTON

V.C.

NOTTINGHAMSHIRE AND DERBYSHIRE REGIMENT

James Upton has the distinction of being the first man from Nottingham to win the Victoria Cross. He was born in the Meadows on the 3rd May 1888, being educated locally before taking employment as a labourer at Mr. W. Rigley's Wagon Works at Bulwell. He enlisted into the Nottinghamshire and Derbyshire Regiment on the 24th July 1906, and after training was posted to India where he served for five years. The Upton family had a long tradition of military service and three of his brothers were already serving in India, one of whom was later killed.

On the 4th November 1914, after the outbreak of the First World War, Upton was sent to France with the Regiment and was soon heavily engaged in the fighting. He was to win his Victoria Cross on the 9th May 1915, at Rouges Bancs, France.

The Citation read

'For the most conspicuous bravery near Rouges Bancs on the 9th May 1915. During the whole day Corporal Upton displayed the greatest courage in rescuing the wounded while exposed to heavy rifle and artillery fire, going close to the enemy's parapet, regardless of his own personal safety. One wounded man was killed by a shell while this non commissioned officer was carrying him. When Corporal Upton was not actually carrying in the wounded he was engaged in bandaging and dressing various cases in front of our parapet, exposed to the enemy's fire.'

The award was Gazetted on the 29th July 1915

He was decorated by King George V at Windsor Castle on the 24th July 1915. He was also given a civic reception in Nottingham where the Mayor presented him with an illuminated address and a purse of gold.

On the 20th July 1915, four days before his investiture at Windsor Castle, James Upton married Jane Chambers at Lincoln and they later had several children. After his discharge from the army in March 1919, he moved with his family to Kingsbury in Middlesex. During the Second World War he served with the 12th Platoon of the Home Guard (Middlesex Regiment) with the rank of Major.

William Upton V.C. died on the 10th August 1949, aged 62 years, at Edgware Hospital and was buried with full military honours at Golders Green Cemetery.

His Victoria Cross and campaign medals were presented to the regiment by his sister-in-law at a reception given at Normanton Barracks, Derby in 1962 and are now on display at the Regimental Museum at Nottingham Castle.

James Upton V.C.

SAMUEL HARVEY
V.C.

YORK AND LANCASTER REGIMENT

Samuel Harvey was born at Basford, Nottingham on the 17th September 1881, the son of a labourer. While he was still young the family moved to Ipswich in Suffolk and after being educated locally he found employment as a farm labourer. In 1905 he enlisted into the 1st Battalion the York and Lancaster Regiment at Doncaster and after training was sent to India, where he served for seven years.

On returning to England he left the regular army. At the outbreak of the First World War however he re-enlisted into his old regiment and, because of his previous military training, was soon sent to France. During his time on the Western Front he was involved in some of the heaviest fighting of the war and was wounded three times, once so badly that he was returned home to convalesce.

Harvey won his Victoria Cross at Big Willie trench on the 29th September 1915.

The Citation read

'During a heavy bombing attack by the enemy and when more bombs were urgently required for our front, Private Harvey volunteered to fetch them, his communication trench was blocked with wounded and reinforcements, and he went backwards and forwards across the open and under intense fire, and succeeded in bringing up no less than thirty boxes of bombs before he was wounded in the head. It was mainly due to Private Harvey's cool bravery in supplying bombs that the enemy was eventually driven back.'

The award was Gazetted on the 18th November 1915

He was decorated by King George V at Buckingham Palace on the 24th January 1917.

On being discharged from the army Samuel Harvey's life became one of both sadness and misfortune. He found difficulty in finding employment due to his wounds. Eventually the Great White Horse Hotel in Ipswich employed him as an ostler and odd-job man and he remained there for many years. He was married in 1944 and for a short time settled down to married life, residing at 10 Adelphi Palace, Ipswich. On the death of his wife Samuel Harvey fell on hard times. He was obliged to take charity and went to live in the local Salvation Army Hostel. To add to his misery, some guttering fell on him and he was crippled. When his plight came to the notice of the public there was an outcry and with the help of donations and the local branch of the Royal British Legion he was found a place at the Heathfields Old Persons Home, Ipswich. Whilst at the home Harvey suffered a fall and was transferred to Stow Lodge Hospital where he died on the 24th September 1960 aged 79. He was buried a few days later with full military honours in the local cemetery.

Samuel Harvey V.C. was a typical example of the fate that befell many men at the conclusion of the Great War. Men who had their lives changed or ruined by the effects of war and were left with little if any help. Samuel Harvey still had a German bullet lodged in his head on the day he died.

Harvey's Victoria Cross and campaign medals were either lost or stolen and to this day have not been recovered. He slept with a miniature of his V.C. under his pillow while he was in hospital and it was found there on the day he died.

Samuel Harvey V.C. sharing a joke with King George V and Queen Mary, at a Garden Party at Buckingham Palace

Captain

SIR CHARLES GEOFFREY VICKERS

V.C.

CROIX-DE-GUERRE (BELGIUM)

NOTTINGHAMSHIRE AND DERBYSHIRE REGIMENT

Charles Geoffrey Vickers was born on the 13th October 1894, the son of Charles Henry Vickers, lace manufacturer. He was educated at Oundle School, Northamptonshire, where he excelled at sports, representing his school at Rugby. On leaving school he spent several months in Germany studying the language before entering Merton College, Oxford in October 1913. While at Oxford, he won a classic exhibition and was reading for honours in moderations and Greats. He also served with the Officer Training Corps.

In September 1914, shortly after the outbreak of the First World War he obtained a commission into the 7th Battalion The Nottinghamshire and Derbyshire Regiment (Robin Hoods) and was posted to France in February 1915. He was involved in the fighting at Ypres and the battle of Loos but it was at the Hohenzoltern Redoubt on the 14th October 1915 that Captain Vickers was to win his Victoria Cross.

His Citation read

'For conspicuous bravery in the Hohenzoltern Redoubt when all his men had been killed or wounded and with only two men available to hand him bombs, Captain Vickers held a barrier for some hours against attacks from the front and flanks. By ordering a second barrier to be built for the safety of the trench, he knowingly cut off his own retreat. He was severely wounded but saved a critical situation.'

The award was Gazetted on the 18th November 1915

He was decorated with his Victoria Cross by King George V at Buckingham Palace on the 15th January 1916.

On his return to Nottingham he was given a civic reception and presented with a gold watch in front of a large cheering crowd in the Market Square. He was promoted to Major and transferred to the 1st Battalion The Lincolnshire Regiment. During his service with the regiment he was again wounded and won the Croix-de-Guerre. (Belgium).

After the war, he qualified as a solicitor and practiced with the firm of Slaughter and May. He continued his sporting interests and was a fine yachtsman coming second in the prestigious Fastnet Race. At the outbreak of the Second World War he was commissioned with the rank of Colonel and was 'specially employed.' He became Deputy Director General of the Ministry of Economic Warfare and was put in charge of economic intelligence and was also a member of the joint intelligence committee to the Chief of Staff.

At the end of the Second World War he continued to practice law and was Knighted in 1946. He played a major part in the foundation of the Mental Health Research Fund contributing much to the development of British psychiatry and became an honorary Fellow of the Royal College of Psychiatry. He sat on many boards and committees and was held in the highest regard by all who knew him. He also published 50 papers and six books on management theory and practice.

Sir Charles Vickers finally died on the 16th March 1982, at the age of 87.

His Victoria Cross and campaign medals are now on display in the Regimental Museum at Nottingham Castle.

Sir Charles Geoffrey Vickers V.C.   Courtesy of The Imperial War Museum Q 85895

Corporal

JOHN CAFFREY

V.C.

RUSSIAN CROSS OF THE ORDER OF ST. GEORGE

YORK AND LANCASTER REGIMENT

John Caffrey was born at Birr, King's Co. (later Co. Offaly) Ireland on the 23rd October 1891. While John was still young, he moved with his family to England and settled in Nottingham. He was educated at St. Mary's Roman Catholic School, Derby Road and was a member of the 12th Nottingham Company of the Boys Brigade. He commenced his military career with the 7th Battalion The Nottinghamshire and Derbyshire Regiment (Robin Hoods) but transferred to his father's old Regiment, the York and Lancaster, in 1910.

He was a good sportsman and won several medals for cross-country running. At the outbreak of the First World War, he was posted to France where he took part in the famous retreat from Mons in 1914 and was involved in many of the major battles during the early part of the war. It was near La Brique, France on the 16th November 1915 that Corporal Caffrey was to win his Victoria Cross.

His Citation read

'For the most conspicuous bravery on the 16th November 1915, near La Brique. A man of the West Yorkshire Regiment had been badly wounded and was lying in the open unable to move and in full view of the enemy being about 300 to 400 yards from the enemy's trenches. Corporal Stirk, Royal Army Medical Corps and Private Caffrey at once started out to rescue him but at the first attempt they were driven back by shrapnel fire. Soon afterwards they started again under close sniping and machine gun fire and succeeded in reaching and bandaging the wounded man, but just as Corporal Stirk had lifted him on Private Caffrey's back, he himself was shot in the head. Private Caffrey put down the wounded man and bandaged Corporal Stirk, and helped him back to safety. He then returned and brought in the man of the West Yorkshire Regiment. He had made three journeys across the open under close and accurate fire and had risked his own life to save others with the utmost coolness and bravery.'

The award was Gazetted on the 22nd January 1916

He was decorated with his Victoria cross by King George V at Buckingham Palace, on the 23rd February 1916. He was also decorated with the Russian Cross of the Order of St. George (fourth class) for bringing in a wounded officer under heavy fire. On his return to Nottingham he was given a civic reception and introduced to cheering crowds in the Old Market Square.

On being discharged from the army, he found employment as a constable with the River Wear Fire Watching Force at Sunderland. On returning to Nottingham, he was employed by the Metropolitan Carriage and Wagon Company with whom he remained until they closed down. After losing his job he spent a period of time unemployed. Caffrey's plight was brought to the attention of Alderman Green, the then Lord Mayor of Nottingham, and due to his personal endeavour employment was found for Caffrey as an assistant public administrator at the Council Offices on Shakespeare Street.

During the Second World War he served as a Company Sergeant-Major with the Sherwood Foresters. At the end of the war he was employed as a Sergeant Commissionaire at Butlin's holiday camp in Filey, Yorkshire. While there he worked with another famous Nottinghamshire Victoria Cross winner, Harry Nicholls, who was the camp boxing instructor.

John Caffrey later moved to Derby, where he took up residence at 41 Wilmot Street. He died on the 26th February 1953 at the Derbyshire Royal Infirmary, aged 62, and was buried with full military honours a few days later.

His Victoria Cross and campaign medals are now on display at the Regimental Museum at Endcliffe Hall, Sheffield.

John Caffrey V.C., photo taken in later life

Sapper

WILLIAM HACKETT

V.C.

ROYAL ENGINEERS

'The most divine-like act of self-sacrifice of which I have read was that of the late Sapper William Hackett, R.E. awarded posthumously the Victoria Cross.' So said Field-Marshall Sir Evelyn Wood V.C. in his famous book on the Victoria Cross.

William Hackett was born in Nottingham on the 11th June 1873, and educated at the local board school before taking employment as a miner. He married a local girl in 1900 and they had a son and a daughter. On losing his job at the pit the family moved to Yorkshire, where Hackett regained employment as a miner.

At the outbreak of the First World War, although above the age for military service, he tried three times to enlist into the York and Lancaster Regiment but was each time rejected. He then applied to join the Royal Engineers and, undoubtedly because he was an experienced miner, they accepted him and he was sent to France attached to the 254th Tunnelling Company. He was involved in much heavy fighting and although being involved in one of the army's most dangerous tasks was always keen and energetic.

It was in June 1916, near Givenchy, France, while Hackett was working on the Shaftesbury Avenue Mine, that he was to win his Victoria Cross and lose his life.

His Citation read

'For the most conspicuous bravery when entombed with four others in a gallery owing to the explosion of an enemy mine after working for twenty hours a hole was made through fallen earth and broken timber and the outside party was met. Sapper Hackett helped three of the men through the hole and could have easily followed, but refused to leave the fourth who had been seriously injured saying, "I am a tunneller and must look after the others first." Meantime the hole was getting smaller yet he still refused to leave his injured comrade. Finally the gallery collapsed and although the rescue party worked desperately for four days, the attempt to reach the two men failed. Sapper Hackett well knowing the nature of sliding earth and the chance against him, deliberately gave his life for his comrade.'

The award was Gazetted on the 5th August 1916

William Hackett's officer Captain G. M. Edwards R.E. wrote to Hackett's widow, 'He has been recommended for the V.C. that simple medal which represents all that is brave and noble.' His Cross was presented to Mrs. Hackett by H.R.H. King George V at Buckingham Palace on the 29th November 1916.

William Hackett's body was never recovered but his name is commemorated on the Ploegsteert Memorial, Belgium and on a memorial tablet on the wall of the Market Hall, Mexborough, Yorkshire.

William Hackett V.C.

Captain
JOHN LESLIE GREEN
V.C.

ROYAL ARMY MEDICAL CORPS

John Leslie Green was born at St. Neots, Huntingdonshire on the 4th December 1888. He was educated at Felsted School, Essex, before moving onto Downing College, Cambridge where he studied to become a doctor and qualified in 1913. While at Cambridge he showed himself to be an outstanding oarsman and rowed for his college. He also excelled at both tennis and golf.

He was House Surgeon at Huntingdon County Hospital when the First World War broke out and was commissioned into the Royal Army Medical Corps. He was at first attached to the 5th South Staffordshire Regiment, before moving to the 1/2 North Midland Field Ambulance Regiment (46th Division). He transferred from this unit and was attached to the 5th Battalion The Nottinghamshire and Derbyshire Regiment. On the 1st January 1916, he married another doctor Miss E. M. Moss but their time together was short and he was soon posted to the Western Front.

The Great Somme offensive started on the 1st July 1916. Captain Green attacked with his Battalion at Foncquevillers and it was during this action that he was to win his Victoria Cross.

His Citation read

'Although himself wounded, he went to the assistance of an officer who had been wounded and was hung up in the enemy's wire entanglements and succeeded in dragging him to a shell hole where he dressed his wounds, notwithstanding that bombs and rifle grenades were thrown at him the whole time. Captain Green then endeavoured to bring the wounded officer into safe cover and had nearly succeeded in doing so when he was killed.'

The award was Gazetted on the 5th August 1916

Captain Green was just one of the 60,000 casulties suffered by the British army on that day, the blackest in British military history. He had been married for only 6 months and was only 28 years old. His Victoria Cross was later presented to his widow by King George V at Buckingham Palace.

Captain Green was buried in the Froncquevillers Military Cemetery, France. His Victoria Cross and campaign medals are now in the possession of the Royal Army Medical Corps.

Captain John Leslie Green V.C., artists impression

Corporal

ROBERT EDWARD RYDER

V.C.

ITALIAN MEDAL FOR MILITARY VALOUR

MIDDLESEX REGIMENT

Robert Edward Ryder was born at Brakspear Road, Harefield, Middlesex on the 17th December 1895 and was educated at the Old Council School before finding employment locally as a labourer. On the 3rd September 1914, shortly after the outbreak of the First World War, he enlisted into the 12th Battalion the Middlesex Regiment. While serving with the army, Ryder established a reputation as a fine sportsman and boxer and went 15 rounds with the great featherweight, Jimmy Wilde, and although out-classed was never knocked down. After training, he was posted to France and won his Victoria Cross at Thiepval, France on the 26th September 1916 when just 20 years old.

His Citation read

'For the most conspicuous bravery and initiative during an attack. His company was held up by heavy rifle fire, and all his officers had become casualties. For want of leadership the attack was flagging. Private Ryder, realized the situation, and without a moment's thought for his own safety dashed absolutely alone at the enemy trench, and by skilful manipulation of his Lewis gun, succeeded in clearing the trench. This very gallant act not only made possible but also greatly inspired the subsequent advance of his comrades, and turned possible failure into success.'

The award was Gazetted on the 25th November 1916

Ryder was also promoted and became the youngest sergeant in the British army.

Two days after winning his Victoria Cross he was seriously wounded in the hip and leg by shell fire and did not regain consciousness until he arrived at Norwich Hospital some considerable time later. On the 29th November 1916, on recovering from his wounds, he was invited to Buckingham Palace where he was decorated by King George V.

It was suggested to Ryder that he remain in England on recruiting duties but he refused, saying that he wanted to be back at the front with his pals. He returned to France just before Christmas, 1916 to find that all his 'pals' had been killed. Shortly after returning to the front line he was captured by a German officer with a perfect English accent. Ryder was not the type of

52

man, however, to take this sort of thing lying down and as soon as the opportunity arose, he and a man from the Royal West Kent Regiment made a run for it and, under a hail of fire, escaped. He had been a prisoner for just 5 minutes!

Bob Ryder not only saw action in France but also in Italy, and while there won the Italian Medal for Military Valour in Bronze, for swimming across the Piave River under the eyes of an enemy patrol, to locate the enemy troops and thus enable his battalion to cross the river safely.

Robert Ryder was finally demobilized in 1919.

At the outbreak of the Second World War he enlisted into the Royal Sussex Regiment as a private but when an officer saw his decorations he was promoted to sergeant. He was engaged on the home front and during this time again distinguished himself when he stopped two horses galloping out of control towards a group of children. After the war he emigrated to Canada and farmed in New Brunswick until 1953 before returning to England and moving to Hucknall, Nottinghamshire. He found employment at Chilwell Ordnance Factory, where he worked until his health began to deteriorate due to the wounds he received during the First World War. Despite fighting his disability with great courage, careful nursing by his wife and numerous hospital visits he died on the 1st December 1978, sixteen days short of his 83rd birthday.

He was buried with full military honours in his home town of Harefield, in the same churchyard as his boyhood hero General Goodlake V.C.

Despite being offered thousands of pounds for his medals, his widow presented them to the Imperial War Museum, London where they are now on view to the nation as a permanent reminder of this very brave man.

Robert Edward Ryder V.C.

Captain

ALBERT BALL

V.C.   D.S.O. (2 bars)   M.C.
FRENCH LEGION d'HONNEUR
RUSSIAN ORDER OF ST. GEORGE

NOTTINGHAMSHIRE AND DERBYSHIRE REGIMENT
attached
ROYAL FLYING CORPS

Albert Ball is without doubt the best known of all the Nottingham's Victoria Cross winners. He was born in Nottingham on the 13th August 1896, the son of a master plumber who later became Lord Mayor of Nottingham. He was educated at both the High School, Nottingham and Trent College, Long Eaton, Derbyshire.

On the 21st September 1914, shortly after the outbreak of the First World War, he enlisted into the ranks of the 7th Battalion of the Nottinghamshire and Derbyshire Regiment, (Robin Hoods), being commissioned a month later on the 29th October. So desperate was Ball to get to the front that he transferred to the North Midland Divisional Cyclist Company but still remained in England throughout 1915. He took up flying in June 1915, paying for private lessons with the Ruffy-Baumann School at Hendon and obtained his Royal Aero Club certificate (No 1898) on the 15th October 1915. He applied for a transfer to the Royal Flying Corps and, on the 22nd January 1916 and after a period of training, received his R.F.C. 'wings.' He was posted to 22 Training Squadron at Gosport as an instructor, but was soon transfered to France joining 13 Squadron in February 1916, flying B.E. 2cs, a slow two-seater aircraft used for reconnaissance and bombing. On the 7th May he was posted to 11 Squadron and given a single-seater Newport-Scout. He soon obtained a reputation as a fine and reckless pilot and on the 26th June destroyed a German observation balloon with a phosphate bomb, for which he was awarded the M.C.

Ball's tally of German aircraft began to mount. On the 16th August he attacked five German Roland two-seaters, shooting one down and forcing another to land. Later on the same day, he again attacked a formation of German aircraft forcing another to land. His total of success against German aircraft increased almost daily. By now he had transfered to 60 Squadron and was given a roving commission to fly and fight as he wished. He was awarded the D.S.O. and Bar and promoted to Flight Commander.

On the 18th November 1916, he attended Buckingham Palace in the company of his family, where he was decorated with the D.S.O. and bar and M.C. by his King, George V. On the 25th November, Ball was awarded a second Bar to his D.S.O., making him the first man in the history of the British Army to be awarded a triple D.S.O.

Although Ball had a reputation as a 'killer' his personality was far-removed from this image. He was a deeply religious man, with a sensitive nature. He looked on his ability as a fighter pilot with a strong sense of duty and never took pleasure from his victories, bearing no animosity towards his German foe. While on leave in Nottingham, he was given a civic reception and cheered by thousands of people in the Old Market Square. In February 1917, as well as being informed that he had been awarded the Russian Order of St. George (4th Class) he was also made an Honorary Freeman of the City of Nottingham, an extraordinary distinction for one so young.

He returned to France and was posted to 56 Squadron, flying S.E. 5s, and continued to increase his reputation and tally of German aircraft. Ball disliked the S.E. 5 and was given a Newport B155 for alternative use. Ball was to lose his life on the 7th May 1917, leading his squadron into an attack on Richthofen's Flying Circus which was at this time led by Lothar Von Richthofen, the Red Baron's brother. During the ensuing dog-fight, Ball's aircraft was seen to dive into a cloudbank in pursuit of Lothar's red Albatross DIII. Neither plane was seen to emerge. Ball's plane was next seen by three German infantry officers coming out of a cloudbank, with a thin plume of black smoke emitting from it, and crashing into a field near the village of Annoevilin. The first person to reach the scene was a French woman by the name of Madame Sieppe Coulon and legend had it that he died in her arms. Mystery has always surrounded Ball's death. Lothar Von Richthofen claimed that he had not shot Ball down, as did a German anti-aircraft gun section. There was no evidence of his plane having been shot down and his body had no combat wounds, his only injuries having been sustained in the crash. There have been numerous theories put forward to explain the young flier's death, but the truth will probably never be known.

On the 9th May 1917, Albert Ball was buried by the Germans with full military honours and the following month it was announced that Captain Albert Ball had been awarded the Victoria Cross.

The Citation read

'Albert Ball, Captain, Nottinghamshire and Derbyshire Regiment and Royal Flying Corps. For the most conspicuous and consistent bravery from the 25th April to the 6th May 1917 during which period Captain Ball took part in twenty-six combats in the air and destroyed eleven hostile aeroplanes, drove two down out of control and forced several others to land.'

The award was Gazetted on the 8th June 1917

His Victoria Cross was presented to his parents by King George V at

Buckingham Palace on the 21st July 1917. The French government also enrolled Ball as a Chevalier de Legion d' Honneur, their highest award for bravery and the American Aero Club awarded him their Diploma and Medal. He was the first British officer ever to receive this honour.

Albert Ball was 20 when he died. He had been credited with at least 44 victories against German aircraft and had more honours for bravery when he died than any other man in the British Army. His body now lies in the Annoeullin Cemetery, France — the only Englishman amongst hundreds of Germans.

A bronze statue of Captain Ball was purchased by public subscription, and erected in the grounds of Nottingham Castle where it still stands. His Victoria Cross, gallantry and campaign medals can now be seen in the Regimental museum of the Nottinghamshire and Derbyshire Regiment at Nottingham Castle.

Albert Ball V.C.

Sergeant
ROBERT JAMES BYE
V.C.

WELSH GUARDS

Robert James Bye was born at 13 Maritime Street, Pontypridd, on the 12th December 1889, the son of Martin and Sarah Bye. He was educated at Penrhiwcelbs School before taking up employment as a collier at Deep Duffryn Colliery. He married in October 1912 and had two sons and two daughters.

He enlisted into the Welsh Guards on the 3rd April 1915 and was posted to France. He soon proved himself during the bitter trench warfare of the Western Front and was promoted to sergeant. He won his Victoria Cross on the 31st July 1917 during the third battle of Ypres during the fighting on the Yser Canal.

The Citation read

'For the most conspicuous bravery. Sergeant Bye displayed the utmost courage and devotion to duty during an attack on the enemy's position. Seeing that the leading waves were being troubled by two enemy blockhouses, he, on his own initiative, rushed at one of them and put the garrison out of action. He then rejoined his company and went forward to assault the second objective. When the troops had gone forward to the attack on the third objective a party was detailed to clear up a line of blockhouses which had been passed. Sergeant Bye volunteered to take charge of this party, accomplished his object and took many prisoners. He subsequently advanced to the third objective capturing a number of prisoners, thus rendering invaluable assistance to the assaulting companies. He displayed throughout the most remarkable initiative.'

(During the action sergeant Bye killed, wounded or captured over seventy of the enemy)

The award was Gazetted on the 6th September 1917

He was decorated with his Victoria Cross by King George V at Buckingham Palace on the 26th September 1917.

Bye was discharged from the Guards on the 1st February 1919 but re-enlisted into the Nottinghamshire and Derbyshire Regiment six months later on the 21st August. He served with them until 1925, after which he returned to the pits, working as a collier at Warsop Main, Firbeck and Welbeck Collieries, in Nottinghamshire. He also worked as a temporary

Police Constable at Mansfield.

During the Second World War he served as a Sergeant-Major with the Nottinghamshire and Derbyshire Regiment, being medically discharged in 1941. He was a member of the Welbeck Abbey British Legion and was a founder member of the Church Warsop and Warsop Vale branches.

He died on the 23rd August 1962, at his daughter's home at Warsop and was buried with full military honours at Warsop cemetery. His Victoria Cross and campaign medals are now on display at the Guards Museum, Wellington Barracks, Knightsbridge, London.

Robert James Bye V.C.   Courtesy of The Imperial War Museum Q 114616

Corporal
ERNEST ALFRED EGERTON
V.C.

NOTTINGHAMSHIRE AND DERBYSHIRE REGIMENT

Ernest Alfred Egerton was born on the 10th November 1897 at Longton, Staffordshire. He was educated at Blurton Church School and on leaving found employment as a miner at the Florence Colliery.

He joined the 3rd Battalion The North Staffordshire Regiment on the 10th November 1915 but transferred to the 16th Battalion The Nottinghamshire and Derbyshire Regiment (Chatsworth Rifles) the following year, while in France.

Corporal Egerton was to win his Victoria Cross south-east of Ypres, Belgium on the 20th September 1917.

His Citation read

'For the most conspicuous bravery, initiative and devotion to duty when during an attack visibility was obscured owing to fog and smoke as a result of which the two leading waves of the attack passed over certain hostile dugouts without clearing them. Enemy rifles assisted by a machine-gun were from these dug-outs inflicting severe casualties on the advancing waves. When volunteers were called for to assist in clearing up the situation, Corporal Egerton at once jumped up and dashed for the dug-outs under heavy fire at short range. He shot in succession a rifleman, a bomber and a gunner, by which time he was supported and 29 of the enemy surrendered. The reckless bravery of the NCO relieved in less than 30 seconds an extremely difficult situation. His gallantry is beyond all praise.'

The award was gazetted on the 26th November 1917

He was decorated by King George V at Buckingham Palace on the 5th December 1917. He also received the personal thanks of the Duke of Devonshire.

Egerton was discharged from the army on the 25th April, 1919 as being permanently unfit for further military service due to the effects of gas. He returned to North Staffordshire and worked as an agent for a firm marketing ex-servicemen's handicrafts before becoming a bus conductor and later a bus inspector. He served with the local defence force during the Second World War and later became a security officer at Rootes Aircraft works at Blythe Bridge before moving to The Staffordshire Potteries at Meir in the same capacity.

He died at his home near Stoke-on-Trent on the 14th February 1967 and was buried at St. Peter's Churchyard, Blythe Bridge with full military honours.

Corporal Egerton's Victoria Cross and campaign medals were presented to the regiment by his widow and are now on display at the Regimental Museum at Nottingham Castle.

Ernest Alfred Egerton V.C.   Courtesy of The Imperial War Museum Q 54252

Sergeant
FRED GREAVES
V.C.

NOTTINGHAMSHIRE AND DERBYSHIRE REGIMENT

Fred Greaves was born on the 16th May 1890 at Killamarsh, Derbyshire, the son of Jude and Edith Greaves. He was educated at the Bonds Main Council School before taking employment as a miner at Markham Colliery. He was a keen cyclist and became the Derbyshire 50 and 100 mile champion. He joined the 9th Battalion The Nottinghamshire and Derbyshire Regiment on the 26th February 1915 and after training was sent first to Egypt and then on to the Dardanelles. During the fighting in Gallipoli, he came to the attention of his senior officers and was promoted. At the conclusion of this disastrous campaign Greaves was sent with his Battalion to France and it was during the Battle of Poel Chappelle near Ypres on the 4th October 1917 that he was to win his Victoria Cross.

His Citation read

'For the most conspicuous bravery, initiative and leadership when his platoon was temporarily held up by machine-gun fire from a concrete stronghold. Seeing that his platoon commander and sergeant were casualties, and realising that unless this post was taken quickly, his men would lose the barrage, Corporal Greaves followed by another non-commissioned officer, rushed forward regardless of his personal safety, reached the rear of the building and bombed the occupants, killing or capturing the garrison and taking four enemy machine-guns. It was solely due to the personal pluck, dash and initiative of this non-commissioned officer that the assaulting line at this point was not held up, and that our troops escaped serious casualties. Later in the afternoon. at a most critical period of the battle when the troops of a flank brigade had given way temporarily under a heavy counter-attack, and when all the officers in his company were casualties, this gallant non-commissioned officer quickly grasped the situation. He collected his men, threw out extra posts on the threatened flank, and opened up rifle and machine-gun fire to infiltrate the advance. The effect of Corporal Greaves' conduct on his men throughout the battle cannot be overestimated, and those under his command responded gallantly to his example.'

The award was gazetted on the 26th November 1917

He was later decorated with his Victoria Cross by King George V at Buckingham Palace.

Fred was not the only brave man in the Greaves family. His brother, 2nd Lieutenant Harry Greaves while serving with the 6th Battalion The Nottinghamshire and Derbyshire Regiment won the D.S.O. and two M.C.'s.

At the end of the war, Fred returned to Markham colliery where he worked as a Deputy. During his time at the pit, he became a member of the colliery's St. John's Ambulance Division and was made an Honorary serving brother of the Venerable Order of Jerusalem, for outstanding service to the division, in 1948. He was also awarded the St. John's Ambulance Long Service and Good Conduct Medal with two bars. He was chairman of both Barlborough and Brimington branches of the Royal British Legion with whom he was continually associated for over 50 years. During the Second World War he served with the local volunteer force.

Fred Greaves died at his home in Brimington, Chesterfield on 11th June 1973. He was the last surviving man of the Nottinghamshire and Derbyshire Regiment to have been decorated with the Victoria Cross.

In accordance with his wishes, his medals were presented to the Regiment by his son and daughter at a civic reception on the 8th December 1973. His Victoria Cross and campaign medals are now on display at the Regimental Museum at Nottingham Castle.

Fred Greaves V.C.   Courtesy of The Imperial War Museum Q 85885

Gunner

CHARLES EDWIN STONE

V.C. M.M.

ROYAL FIELD ARTILLERY

Charles Edwin Stone was born at Street Lane, Denby, near Belper on the 4th February 1889 and was one of 13 children. He was educated at the Pottery School, Belper before taking up employment as a miner at Denby and Saltwood collieries.

He enlisted into the Royal Field Artillery as a gunner in September 1914, and after training was sent to France where he joined 'C' battery, 85th Brigade. He suffered a personal tragedy in 1917 when his brother was killed in action. In October 1917 Gunner Stone was awarded the M.M. for treating a wounded man regardless of his own safety during a heavy bombardment and less than six months later on the 21st March 1918 at Caponne Farm, France he won the Victoria Cross.

His Citation read

'For the most conspicuous bravery, initiative and devotion to duty. After working hard at his gun for six hours under heavy gas and shell fire, Gunner Stone was sent back to the rear section with an order. He delivered the order, and voluntarily, under a very heavy barrage, returned with a rifle to the forward position to assist in holding up the enemy on a sunken road. Lying in the open about 100 yards from the enemy and under very heavy machine-gun fire, he calmly and effectively shot the enemy until ordered to retire. He then took up a position on the right flank of the two rear guns and held the enemy at bay, though they again and again attempted to outflank the guns. During this period one of the enemy managed to break through and regardless of fierce machine-gun fire raging at the time, Gunner Stone rushed after him and killed him, thereby saving the guns' flank. Later he was one of the party which captured the machine-gun and four prisoners who, in the dusk, had got round to the rear of the gun position. This most gallant act undoubtedly saved the detachment serving the guns. Gunner Stone's behaviour throughout the whole day was beyond all praise and his magnificent example and fine work through these critical periods undoubtedly kept the guns in action, thereby holding up the enemy on the battle zone at the most crucial movement.'

The award was Gazetted on the 22nd May 1918

He was decorated by King George V at Buckingham Palace on the 22nd June 1918.

On his return to Belper he was given a civic reception and carried in an open Landau drawn by a pair of grey horses in front of hundreds of cheering spectators. He was presented with a gold watch and chain and a £100 worth of war bonds. The people of Ripley, not to be outdone, also gave Gunner Stone a civic reception and presented him with a further £100 worth of war bonds.

After his discharge from the army in 1919 he returned to Belper and continued to work at the Saltwood Colliery. In 1923 he moved to Ashbourne and worked at Heywood Farm for a Mr. Clifford Etches. While there he was again involved in an act of bravery when he saved the life of a woman whose dress had caught fire.

His health began to fail due to his war service and he was admitted to the City Hospital, Derby, where he died on the 29th August 1952 at the age of 61. He was buried with full military honours in his mother's grave in Belper Cemetery.

His Victoria Cross and campaign medals are now with the Royal Artillery Institute in Woolwich.

Charles Edwin Stone V.C.

Sergeant

WILLIAM GREGG

V.C.   D.C.M.   M.M.

RIFLE BRIGADE

William Gregg was the first man to be awarded all three principal awards for gallantry during the First World War.

He was born at Heanor, Derbyshire on the 27th January 1890, and was educated at Heanor Mundy Street School. On leaving school, he became a miner at the Shipley Colliery. Shortly after the outbreak of the First World War he enlisted into the Rifle Brigade and travelled with them to France in May, 1915. He quickly established a reputation as a fearless soldier and was to be heavily decorated.

On the 4th February 1917, Gregg was awarded the Military Medal for leading a daring daylight raid on the German trenches and obtaining much useful information. He was also promoted to Corporal.

On the 30th November 1917, Gregg was again in the thick of the fighting. The Germans attacked his battalion in large numbers and seeing the battalion on the left flank being hard-pressed, Gregg carried several messages across a road swept by machine-gun fire and in so doing was cut-off from his company. He then led a counter-attack killing and driving off the enemy. For this action he was awarded the Distinguished Conduct Medal and the following December promoted to the rank of sergeant.

Sergeant Gregg was awarded the Victoria Cross for his actions on the 8th May 1918 at Bucquoy, France.

The Citation read

'William Gregg D.C.M., M.M. No. 6522 Sergeant Rifle Brigade. For the most conspicuous bravery and brilliant leadership in action. Two companies of his unit attacked the enemy's outpost position without artillery preparation. Sergeant Gregg was with the right company which came under heavy fire from the right flank as it advanced. All the officers with the company were hit. He at once took command of the attack. He rushed an enemy post and personally killed the entire machine-gun team and captured the gun and four men in a dug-out nearby. He then rushed another post, killed two men and captured another. In spite of heavy casualties he reached his objective and started consolidating the position. By this prompt and effective action this gallant N.C.O. saved the situation at a critical time and ensured the success of the attack. Later Sergeant Gregg's party was driven back by an enemy counter-attack but, reinforcements coming up, he led a charge, personally bombed a hostile machine-gun and killed the crew and captured the gun. Once again he

66

was driven back. He led another successful attack and hung onto the position until ordered by his company commander to withdraw, although under very heavy rifle and machine-gun fire for several hours, Sergeant Gregg displayed throughout the greatest coolness and contempt of danger walking about encouraging his men and setting a magnificent example.'

The award was Gazetted on the 28th June 1918

He was decorated by King George V at Frohen-le-Grand, France, on the 9th August 1918. (See photograph below).

After the war he returned to Heanor and resumed work as a miner. He played full-back for Heanor Athletic Football Club and was involved in the coaching of their youth team. So popular was 'Bill' that local admirers subscribed to the purchase of a valuable cup which was inscribed to commemorate his gallant deeds and to this day is known as the 'Gregg Cup.'

During the Second World War he served with the Sherwood Foresters, National Defence Company, but was discharged in 1941 having reached the upper age limit. He next served on the ferries and was involved in bringing back survivors from the Dieppe raid.

After the war he returned to Heanor and continued to work at Shipley Colliery until 1959 when he was forced to retire due to ill-health. He died in Heanor Memorial Hospital on the 9th August 1969, aged 79, and was buried with full military honours in the local cemetery.

William Gregg V.C. receiving his medal from King George V
Courtesy of The Imperial War Museum Q 11133

Lieutenant Colonel

CHARLES EDWARD HUDSON

V.C.　　C.B.　　D.S.O.　　M.C.

CROIX-DE-GUERRE (French)

ITALIAN SILVER MEDAL FOR VALOUR

NOTTINGHAMSHIRE AND DERBYSHIRE REGIMENT

Charles Edward Hudson was born at Derby on the 29th May 1892 the son of Lieutenant-Colonel H. E. Hudson. He was educated at Sherborne School, Dorset and the Royal Military College, Sandhurst. In 1912, he travelled to Ceylon where he ran a tea plantation before returning to England at the outbreak of the First World War. He was commissioned as a temporary 2nd Lieutenant into the Nottinghamshire and Derbyshire Regiment and sent to France.

He quickly established himself as a good and efficient officer and was promoted. He also earned a reputation as an outstandingly brave man and won two D.S.O.s, the M.C. the French Croix-de-Guerre, the Italian Medal for Military Valour and was mentioned in despatches no less than four times.

Hudson was to win his Victoria Cross on the 15th June 1918 while serving as an acting Lieutenant-Colonel with the 11th Battalion on the Asiago Plateau in Italy.

The Citation read

'For the most conspicuous bravery and devotion to duty when his battalion was holding the right front sector during an attack on the British front. The shelling had been very heavy on the right, the trench destroyed, and considerable casualties had occurred, and all the officers on the spot were killed or wounded. This enabled the enemy to penetrate our front line. The enemy pushed their advance as far as the support line which was the key to our front flank, the situation demanded immediate action. Lieutenant-Colonel Hudson, recognizing its gravity at once collected various headquarters details, such as orderlies, servants, runners, etc., and, together with some allies, personally led them up the hill. Driving the enemy down the hill towards our front line he again led a party of about five up the trench, where there were about 200 enemy, in order to attack them from one flank. He then with two men got out of the trench and rushed the position, shouting to the enemy to surrender, some of whom did. He was then severely wounded by a bomb which exploded on his foot. Although in great pain, he gave directions for the counter-attack to be

68

continued, and this was done successfully, about 100 prisoners and six machine-guns being taken. Without doubt the high courage and determination displayed by Lieutenant-Colonel Hudson saved a serious situation and had it not been for his quick determination in organizing the counter-attack a large number of the enemy would have dribbled through, and counter-attack on a large scale would have been necessary to restore the situation.

The award was Gazetted on the 11th July 1918

He was decorated by King George V at Buckingham Palace on the 18th September 1918. He was also decorated with the Italian Medal for Military Valour.

In April 1919 he was sent to North Russia as a Brigade Major to help suppress the Bolshevik Revolution and while there was again mentioned in despatches twice.

On his return from Russia, he married and took the post of Adjutant to the local Militia, a position he held until 1923. He was also the Military Adviser to the Federated Malay States and the Chief Instructor at Sandhurst. Subsequently he commanded the 2nd Battalion the King's Own Scottish Borderers and the 2nd Infantry Brigade. During the Second World War he was present at Dunkirk and was created a C.B. The Second World War also brought tragedy when one of his sons was killed in action.

Between 1944 and 1946 he was ADC to King George VI and became Deputy Lieutenant for the county of Devon as well as being a Justice of the Peace. He died suddenly in the Scilly Isles on the 4th April 1959 a month short of his sixty seventh year. His body was returned to Devon and later buried in Denbury Churchyard, near Newton Abbot, Devon.

Charles Edward Hudson V.C.

Lieutenant Colonel (Revd)

BERNARD WILLIAM VANN

V.C.   M.C. and Bar

CROIX-DE-GUERRE (French)

NOTTINGHAMSHIRE AND DERBYSHIRE REGIMENT

Bernard William Vann was born in Rushden, Northamptonshire on the 9th July 1887, the son of Alfred George Collins Vann M.A., Head Master of Chichele College, Higham Ferrers. He was educated at Chichele College, before going onto Jesus College, Cambridge, where he was a hockey blue. He took his degree in 1910 and was ordained deacon in 1912. He became Chaplain and assistant master at Wellingborough School and at the outbreak of the First World War, he applied for an Army Chaplaincy. After waiting for some time for a position he became impatient and took a commission into the 8th Battalion The Nottinghamshire and Derbyshire Regiment. He was a man of outspoken expressions and while still only a Second Lieutenant was involved in a heated argument with the Army Commander, General Allenby.

He won the Military Cross in 1915, for saving a serious situation during a German attack with a flame thrower and restoring confidence at a critical moment. In June 1916, he was promoted to Captain and later to Major. In September 1916, although suffering continuous agony from neuritis caused by one of his many wounds, he insisted in leading his company in a raid on an enemy trench and in so doing killed and captured several Germans. For this action he was awarded a bar to his Military Cross.

In February 1917, he was awarded the Croix-de-Guerre with Palm (French) and in the October of that year was promoted to Acting Lieut-Colonel. He was married in December 1917 at St. Paul's, Knightsbridge to Doris Victoria Beck and they had one son, born after his father's death on the 2nd June 1919.

Lieut-Colonel Vann was to win his Victoria Cross at Bellenglise and Lehaucourt, France on the 29th September 1918.

His Citation read

'He led his battalion with great skill across the Canal Du Nord through a very thick fog and under heavy fire from field and machine-guns. On reaching the high ground above Bellenglise, the whole attack was held up by fire of all descriptions from the front and right flank. Realising that everything depended on the advance going forward with the barrage Lieut-Colonel Vann rushed up to the firing line and with the greatest gallantry led the line forward. By his prompt action and absolute contempt

70

for danger the whole situation changed, the men were encouraged and the line swept forward. Later he rushed a field-gun single-handed and knocked out three of the detachment. The success of the day was in no small degree due to the spendid gallantry and fine leadership displayed by this officer.'

The award was Gazetted on the 14th December 1918

On the 3rd October 1918, just four days after winning his Victoria Cross and while leading yet another attack against an enemy position, Colonel Vann was killed by a sniper's bullet. He was buried the same day and now lies in the Bellicourt British Cemetery, France. Colonel Vann had been in the thick of the fighting from the beginning of the war to almost its conclusion. He had been wounded at least eight times and decorated for bravery four times.

His Victoria Cross was presented to his widow by King George V at Buckingham Palace on the 26th November 1919.

His Victoria Cross and other medals are now on display in the Regimental Museum at Nottingham Castle.

Bernard William Vann V.C.

Sergeant

WILLIAM HENRY JOHNSON
V.C.
LEGION OF HONOUR (French)

NOTTINGHAMSHIRE AND DERBYSHIRE REGIMENT

William Henry Johnson was the only known campanologist to win the Victoria Cross during the First World War. He was born at Worksop, Nottinghamshire on the 15th October 1890 and educated locally before being employed as a miner at Manton Colliery. Johnson spent most of his spare time at the local church where he was a keen and accomplished bell-ringer. At the outbreak of the First World War he enlisted into the Nottinghamshire and Derbyshire Regiment and was sent to France. While there, he was involved in the heavy fighting on the Western Front and quickly promoted to Sergeant.

On the 3rd October 1918 while engaged in heavy fighting with his battalion at Ramicourt he won the Victoria Cross.

His Citation read

'For the most conspicuous bravery at Ramicourt on the 3rd October 1918 when his platoon was held up by a nest of machine-guns at very close range. Sergeant Johnson worked his way forward under very heavy fire and single-handed charged the post, bayoneting several gunners and capturing two machine-guns. During his attack he was severely wounded by a bomb but continued to lead his men forward. Shortly afterwards the line was once more held by machine-guns. Again he rushed forward and attacked the post single-handed. With wonderful courage he bombed the garrison, put the guns out of action and captured the teams. He showed throughout the most exceptional gallantry and devotion to duty.'

The award was Gazetted on the 14th December 1918

At Johnson's Parish church a peal of bells was rung to honour his award and the French awarded him the Legion of Honour. He was the last member of the Regiment to win the Victoria Cross during the First World War.

After his discharge in 1919 he was employed as a check weighman for a coal and iron company but later became a deputy at Manton Colliery. He became the licensee at the 'Mason's Arms' in Worksop and was the Chairman of the Worksop branch of the Royal British Legion. He moved to Arnold in 1928 where he became the steward of the ex-servicemen's

72

club until 1938 when the club burnt down. He was also a bell-ringer at St. Paul's church in Daybrook. During the Second World War he served with the Home Guard until ill-health forced him to retire.

Johnson died aged 54 at 33 Nelson Road, Arnold, on the 23rd April 1945 and was buried with full military honours at Redhill Cemetery, Nottingham.

His Victoria Cross and campaign medals are now on display at the Regimental Museum at Nottingham Castle.

William Henry Johnson V.C.

Captain

GODFREY MEYNELL

V.C.   M.C.

QUEEN VICTORIA'S OWN CORPS OF GUIDES
12th FRONTIER FORCE REGIMENT
INDIAN ARMY

One expects Victoria Crosses to be won in times of war but, during the relatively peaceful times between them, it is rare. One such award was made to Captain Godfrey Meynell for his actions during troubles in the Mohmand Country, India.

Godfrey Meynell was born at Meynell Langley, Derbyshire on the 20th May 1904, the son of Brigadier-General Godfrey Meynell. He was educated privately at Noris Hill School before being elected to Eton as a King's scholar in 1917. From Eton he went to Sandhurst where he did well, passing out thirteenth, and later travelled to India to join his father's old regiment, The King's Shropshire Light Infantry.

He was a gifted linguist and specialised in the languages of North India and became an interpreter in Hindustani and Pushtu. He fell in love with India and its people and in 1926 transferred to the Corps of Guides. In 1930 he served for an interval with the Tochi Scouts, where he was badly wounded during his first action, being shot through the back while getting his men away from an ambush. He transferred to the South Waziristan Scouts before rejoining the Guides as Adjutant in 1931.

The following year he won the Military Cross for laying a very successful night ambush while escorting the Chitral Relief Expedition.

He married in 1933 and had two sons.

Captain Meynell was to win his Victoria Cross during a battle in the Mohmand Country in September 1935.

The Citation read

'On September 29th 1935, while operating against Mohand tribesmen in the attack on point 4080, Captain Meynell was Adjutant of the battalion. In the final phase of the attack the battalion commander was unable to get information from his most forward troops. Captain Meynell went forward to ascertain the situation and found the forward troops on the objective but involved in a struggle against an enemy vastly superior in numbers. Seeing the situation he at once took over command of the men in this area. The enemy, by this time was closing in on the position from three sides.

Captain Meynell had at his disposal two Lewis guns and about 30 men.

74

Although this party was maintaining heavy and accurate fire on the advancing enemy, the overwhelming numbers of the latter succeeded in reaching the position. Both Lewis guns were damaged beyond repair and a fierce hand-to-hand struggle commenced. During the struggle Captain Meynell was mortally wounded and all his men were either killed or wounded.

Throughout the action, Captain Meynell endeavoured by all means to communicate the situation to headquarters but determined to hold on at all costs and encouraged his men to fight with him to the last. By so doing, he inflicted on the enemy very heavy casualties which prevented them from exploiting their success.

The fine example Captain Meynell set to his men, coupled with his determination to hold the position to the last, maintained the traditions of the army and reflect the highest credit on the fallen officer and his comrades.'

The award was Gazetted on the 24th December 1935

His body was brought back from the field and buried with full military honours in the Guides Cemetery at Mardan, where he was laid to rest next to his great friend Tony Randall who was killed in the same action.

His Victoria Cross was presented to the Captain's widow by King Edward VIII at Buckingham Palace on the 14th July 1936. It was the only Victoria Cross awarded during his short reign.

There is a memorial to Captain Meynell V.C. in Kirk Langley Parish Church, Derbyshire.

Godfrey Meynell V.C.

Corporal

HARRY NICHOLLS

V.C.

GRENADIER GUARDS

Harry Nicholls was, without doubt, one of the best remembered and most popular winners of the Victoria Cross in Nottingham. He was born on Hope Street, The Meadows, Nottingham on the 21st April 1918 and was one of thirteen children. He was educated at the Bosworth Road School, before being employed by Burroughs Adding Machines Ltd., on Arkwright Street. He was an excellent all-round sporstman and was not only a very strong swimmer, but also played football for Whithead's Athletic. He learned to box at the Y.M.C.A. club on London Road and it was in this sport that he was to later excel. He joined the 3rd Battalion, The Grenadier Guards on the 6th June 1936, and while in the Guards was encouraged to continue with his boxing. In 1938 he won the Heavyweight Championship of the British Army at the Albert Hall, and then the Imperial Services Heavyweight title at the Express Hall, Earls Court, London. In April 1937, he married Miss Connie Carroll from Sneinton and they had a baby daughter.

At the outbreak of the Second World War Lance-Corporal Nicholls was sent to France with the first draft of the British Expeditionary Force and was soon heavily engaged against the enemy. He won his Victoria Cross at the River Escourt, Belgium, on the 21st May 1940.

His Citation read

'On the 21st May 1940 Lance-Corporal Nicholls was commanding a section in the right forward platoon of his company when the company was ordered to counter-attack. At the very start of the advance he was wounded in the arm by shrapnel but continued to lead his section forward. As the company came over a small ridge the enemy opened heavy machine-gun fire at close range. Lance-Corporal Nicholls realising the danger to the company immediately seized a Bren-gun and dashed forward towards the machine-guns firing from the hip. He succeeded in silencing first one machine-gun and then two others, in spite of being again severely wounded.

Lance-Corporal Nicholls then engaged the German infantry massed behind causing many casualties and continued to fire until he had no more ammunition left. He was wounded at least four times in all, but absolutely refused to give in. There is no doubt that his gallant action was *instrumental in enabling his company to reach its objective and in causing the enemy to fall back across the river Scheldt. He has since been reported killed.'*

The award was Gazetted on the 30th July 1940

Mrs. Nicholls received the Victoria Cross from King George VI at Buckingham Palace on the 6th August 1940. It was one of the first two Victoria Crosses of the Second World War.

What followed can only be described as one of the more bizarre stories to surround the history of the Victoria Cross. Some years after the death of Lance Corporal Nicholls had been presumed, news was received that in-fact he was not dead but was a prisoner-of-war in Germany. After the battle, Nicholls had been treated by a German medical officer and transferred to a military hospital. From there he had been transferred to various prisoner-of-war camps, making information on his welfare difficult for the Red Cross to obtain. Nicholls was finally interned in Stalag XXA and became the camp's physical training instructor and coached the camp boxing team. He was notified of his award by the Camp Commandant on the personal permission of Adolf Hitler. The whole camp paraded and cheered the news. Harry Nicholls was liberated by the Americans in May 1945 and flown home by Lancaster to be reunited with his family.

On the 22nd June 1945 he attended Buckingham Palace in company with his wife and daughter to be decorated by King George VI. It was one of the rare occasions when the Victoria Cross has been presented twice.

Harry Nicholls was discharged from the army in April 1946. As a result of his wounds, he found adjusting to civilian life hard. He was employed as a boxing instructor at Butlin's camp in Filey for a short while, where he worked with another Nottingham V.C. winner Sergeant Caffrey. On returning to Nottingham, he found it hard to keep employment due to his constant visits to the hospital to have his old wounds treated. He was offered employment in Rhodesia, and while flying out there the plane in which he was flying was thought to have crashed and Harry Nicholls was again presumed to have been killed. In fact the plane had made a forced landing and Harry was alive and well. He was employed as a commissionaire in a Salisbury bank and the family began to make a new life for themselves in the country. While on holiday in England, however, Harry was again taken ill and was unable to return to Rhodesia. Illness dogged the rest of his life and made it impossible for him to hold down a steady job. He married for a second time and moved to Margate with his new wife Grace. The Grenadier Guards on hearing of his plight found him a Grenadier Guards Association flat in Leeds where he died aged 60, on the 11th September 1975. His body was returned to Nottingham and was buried with full military Honours at Wilford Hill Cemetery.

Harry Nicholls never recovered from the wounds he received while winning his Victoria Cross. As in so many of these cases his brave actions saved many lives, but the resultant poor health caused by his wounds disrupted the rest of his life.

The Grenadier Guards, at a ceremony at Bosworth Junior School, presented the school with a plaque commemorating Harry Nicholls V.C., their bravest pupil.

His Victoria Cross and campaign medals are now in the possession of the Grenadier Guards and can be seen at their Regimental Museum in London.

Harry Nicholls V.C.   Courtesy of The Imperial War Museum 1/1340

Captain
ROBERT St. VINCENT SHERBROOK
V.C.   C.B.   D.S.O.

ROYAL NAVY

Robert St. Vincent Sherbrook was without doubt one of the most outstanding naval officers this country has ever produced. He was born at Oxton Hall, near Newark, Nottinghamshire, on the 8th January 1901 in the home his ancestors had occupied since the 15th century.

He attended Osborne College in September 1913 and was promoted to Midshipman on New Years Day 1917. He first saw service during the First World War, at the end of which he was one of the officers selected to attend Cambridge University to recover some 'civilising influence.' In 1921 he was promoted to Lieutenant and in 1924 joined the battleship 'Iron Duke.' He married Rosemary Neville at St. George's, Hanover Square, London in 1929 and they had two daughters.

During the Spanish Civil War he saw service as a commander on H.M.S. Vanoc and during the 'Altmark incident' was in command of H.M.S. Cossack. He won the D.S.O. at the second battle of Narvik on the 13th April 1940 when Cossack together with nine other destroyers cleared a fjord of eight German warships.

It was in December 1942 while escorting convoy JW51B around the North Cape in command of H.M.S. Onslow that he was to win his Victoria Cross.

The Citation read

'Captain Sherbrook, in H.M.S. Onslow, was the senior officer in command of the destroyers escorting an important convoy bound for North Russia. On the morning of December 31st 1942 off the North Cape, he made contact with a greatly superior enemy force which was attempting to destroy the convoy. Captain Sherbrook led his destroyers into the attack and closed with the enemy. Four times the enemy tried to attack the convoy but were forced each time to withdraw behind a smoke screen to avoid the threat of torpedoes and each time Captain Sherbrook pursued him and drove him outside gun range of the convoy and towards our covering forces. The engagements lasted about two hours, but after the first 40 minutes H.M.S. Onslow was hit and Captain Sherbrook was seriously wounded in the face and temporarily lost the use of one eye. Nevertheless he continued to direct the ships under his command until further hits on his own ships compelled him to disengage but not until he was satisfied that the next senior officer had assumed control. It was only then that he agreed to leave the bridge for medical attention, and until the

80

convoy was out of danger he insisted on receiving all reports of the action. His courage, his fortitude and his cool and prompt decisions inspired all around him. By his leadership and example the convoy was saved from damage and was brought safely to its destination.'

The award was Gazetted on the 12th January 1943

As a result of Sherbrook's action the convoy got through with its urgently-needed supplies. Hitler was furious and Raeder, Commander-in-Chief of the German Navy, resigned. After receiving treatment for his injuries he returned to Scapa Flow where he was 'cheered in' by the home fleet.

He was decorated by King George VI at Buckingham Palace in June 1943.

In spite of losing the sight in his left eye, he returned to duty and continued with his distinguished naval career being promoted to the rank of Rear-Admiral in 1951. He was made a C.B. in 1953 and a Gentleman Usher to the Scarlet Rod. He retired, due to ill health, in 1954 and later became High Sheriff of Nottingham as well as being a well-known and popular magistrate.

He died at his home in Oxton on the 13th June 1972 and was interred at the Parish Church. The flag that 'Onslow' was flying on the day Captain Sherbrook won his Victoria Cross, can still be seen in Oxton Church and serves as a permanent memorial to a very brave man.

Robert St. Vincent Sherbrook V.C. Courtesy of The Imperial War Museum HU 1920

Captain
JOHN HENRY BRUNT
V.C.   M.C.

NOTTINGHAMSHIRE AND DERBYSHIRE REGIMENT
attached
LINCOLN REGIMENT

John Henry Brunt was born at Priest Weston, Chirbury, Shropshire, on the 6th December 1922 and educated at the Welsh Frankton School, where he had a reputation for being a bit reckless. He not only got himself involved in fights with local gypsies but was often found by enraged farmers, riding an assortment of animals bare-back around their fields.

He continued his education at Ellesmere College and entered Meynell House. He excelled at sport and became a sergeant in the College Cadet Force.

In 1941 he left school and joined the Royal West Kent Regiment where he became a physical training instructor and represented his regiment at Rugby, boxing and athletics. His abilities soon brought him to the attention of the commanding officer and he was sent for Officer Cadet Training after which he was commissioned into the Nottinghamshire and Derbyshire Regiment. He was posted to North Africa and was to take part in the campaigns both there and in Italy, being wounded four times.

Brunt's reckless bravery soon became a legend amongst the men who served with him. He was promoted to Captain and on the 15th December 1943, as a result of a daring raid against an enemy strong-hold and for attempting to save a wounded man, he was awarded the Military Cross. Part of an Italian Stream became known as 'Brunts Brook' because of the amount of times he crossed it to attack the enemy.

He was posted to the 6th Battalion The Lincolnshire Regiment while still serving in Italy and it was while attached to them that he won his Victoria Cross.

The Citation read

'In Italy on the 9th December 1944, while his platoon was holding a vital sector of the line it was attacked by the enemy in overwhelming numbers causing heavy casualties, he rallied his remaining men and held his position until ordered to retire. He stayed behind to give covering fire until his men were safe before he himself moved back. When the situation eased, he returned and rescued the wounded. Later in the day he stood on the turret of a tank and directed fire at the advancing enemy. He then moved forward on foot and stalked the enemy with a machine-gun, forcing them to retire.'

The award was Gazetted on the 8th February 1945

War throws up many cruel ironies. Having survived many savage engagements Captain Brunt was killed by a stray shell the day after he had won his Victoria Cross, while he was having a quiet cup of tea at his platoon H.Q. He was buried with full military honours at the Faenza War Cemetery, Italy.

His Victoria Cross and campaign medals are still with the family

John Henry Brunt V.C.   Courtesy of The Imperial War Museum HU 2011

ACKNOWLEDGEMENTS

I am deeply indebted to the following people for all their time, help and support:

Peter Naylor, without whose support and advice this book would never have been written or finished.

David Beeston, who examined the text.

Dr. B. Hilton, Dr. J. Lonsdale my tutors at Cambridge, to whom I owe so much.

The late Canon William Lummis MC, for his support and encouragement.

Derek Oldershaw, who introduced me to the fascinating subject of medal collecting.

Dennis Ingle, for the use of his shop and books, and the provision of endless cups of coffee.

Major J. Creamer, of the Notts and Derby Regimental Museum.

Captain Double and Colour Sergeant V. Axworthy, Grenadier Guards.

Royal Army Medical Corps Museum.

Don Scott, York and Lancaster Regimental Museum.

Staff of the Nottinghamshire Central Library Local Studies Department.

The Director and Staff of the Imperial War Museum for allowing me access to the comprehensive files of the late Canon Lummis MC.

Staff of the Reading Room, and courtesy of the Director of the National Army Museum, London.

Captain P. J. Gardner V.C., M.C. for writing the foreword to the book.

Nicci Radford, for typing the first draft.

Mr. A Whybrow, Middlesex Regiment.

The Commonwealth War Graves Commission, for information relating to memorials and graves.

Stephen Garnett, *This England Magazine*.

Simon Jones, and the Royal Engineers Museum, Chatham.

Colin, Julia, and Ashley McCrery, my parents and brother, for having put up with me for the past 35 years.

Gordon Hull, for his photographs of the Notts. and Derby winners of the Victoria Cross.

Mr. P. Kemp, Department of Photographs, Imperial War Museum, for his time in searching for photographs of the recipients.

Mr. Michael G. Morris, Chairman of J. H. Hall and Sons Ltd., for accepting the book for publication.

Richard Nash, Stephen Prohaska, and Peter Montague-Fuller, without whose friendship the last two years would have been much harder.

Mr. Ron Braisby and the Photographic Department of the Nottingham Evening Post.

Christopher Kelly, soon to be a Fellow Elect of Pembroke College Cambridge, and without whose help I would never have got through.

David Turner, for his help and friendship during many projects in Cambridge.

Alan Clay, my friend and fellow collector.

BIBLIOGRAPHY

Abbott, P. E. and Tamplin, J.M.A., British Gallantry Awards
(Guinness Superlatives, London 1971)

Bowyer, Chaz, For Valour — The Air V.C.s
(William Kimber, London 1978)

Bowyer, Chaz, Albert Ball V.C.,
(William Kimmber and Co. Ltd., London 1977)

Crook, M. J., The Evolution of the Victoria Cross
(Midas Books, Tunbridge Wells 1975)

Forsythe-Jauch, Coln. W. E. I. O.B.E., Tennuci, Colin A. V. The Medical Victoria Crosses
(Arrow Press, Aldershot, Hants.)

Gordon, Major L. L., British Battles and Medals
(Spink and Son Ltd., fourth edition 1971)

Imperial War Museum. V.C. Files of the late Cannon Lummis M.C.

James, Brig. E. A. O.B.E., T.D., British Regiments 1914-18
(Samson Books, London 1978)

Lucas-Phillips, Brigadier C.E., Victoria Cross Battles of the Second World War
(Heinemann, London 1973)

National Army Museum. Files on recipients of the V.C.

Notts. and Derbys. Regt. Files on Regimental winners of the V.C.

Nottingham Central Library. Files on local V.C. winners.

O'Moore Creagh, Sir V.C., Humphris E.M., The Victoria Cross 1856-1920
(J. B. Hayward and Son 1985)
Originally published in 1920

Percival, John. For Valour, The Victoria Cross Courage In Action
(Methuen London Ltd. 1985)

Perkins, Roger. The Kashmir Gate, Lieutenant Home and the Delhi V.C.s
(Picton Publishing 1983)

Roe, F. Gordon, The Bronze Cross
(P. R. Gawthorn, London 1945)

Smyth, Sir John V.C. The Story of the Victoria Cross
(Frederick Muller, London 1962)

The Register of the Victoria Cross
(This England Books, Cheltenham, Gloucestershire 1981)

Winton, John, The Victoria Cross At Sea
(Michael Joseph, London 1978)

LIST OF ABBREVIATIONS

V.C.	Victoria Cross
K.C.B.	Knights Commander of the most Honourable Order of the Bath
C.B.	Knights Companion of the most Honourable Order of the Bath
D.S.O.	Distinguished Service Order
M.C.	Military Cross
D.C.M.	Distinguished Conduct Medal
M.M.	Military Medal
N.C.O.	Non-Commissioned Officer

INDEX